Friendship Fires

Friendship Fires

Sam Cook

Illustrations by Terry Maciej

University of Minnesota Press

Minneapolis • London

Grateful acknowledgment is made to the *Duluth News-Tribune* for permission to reprint these stories and columns, which originally appeared in that newspaper.

Originally published in hardcover by Pfeifer-Hamilton, 1999
First University of Minnesota Press edition, 2003

Published by the University of Minnesota Press
111 Third Avenue South, Suite 290
Minneapolis, MN 55401-2520
http://www.upress.umn.edu

Library of Congress Cataloging-in-Publication Data

Cook, Sam
    Friendship fires / Sam Cook ; illustrated by Terry Maciej.— 1st University of Minnesota Press ed.
    p. cm.
Originally pubished: Duluth : Pfeifer-Hamilton, 1999.
A collection of stories and columns originally appearing in the Duluth news
    tribune.
ISBN 0-8166-4266-4 (pbk. : alk. paper)
1. Outdoor life—Minnesota—Duluth Region—Anecdotes. 2. Duluth Region (Minn.)—Description and travel—Anecdotes. 3. Duluth Region (Minn.)—Social life and customs—20th century—Anecdotes. 4. Cook, Sam—Anecdotes. I. Title.

F614.D8C756 2003
977.6'771053—dc21

                                                            2003040210

Printed in the United States of America on acid-free paper

The University of Minnesota is an equal-opportunity educator and employer.

12 11 10 09 08 07 06 05 04 03   10 9 8 7 6 5 4 3 2 1

For Phyllis, Emily, and Grant

Acknowledgments

As always, there is Phyllis. It must not be easy for her, being married to someone who is gone a lot. I thank her for her understanding when we're apart and her partnership when we're together.

Emily and Grant, too. I think I miss them when I'm gone more than they miss me; but then, a person never knows for sure.

All of these columns and stories appeared first in the *Duluth News-Tribune,* which has once again graciously granted permission to reprint them. I thank my editor at the *News-Tribune,* Connie Wirta, whose touches smoothed the rough edges on my work.

I came to know artist Terry Maciej when we did a duck hunt together in the country north and west of Grand Rapids. His sensitivity to the landscape and his eye for details are evident in the scratchboard drawings that illustrate these pages.

I don't know exactly how to thank the many other writers whose works have influenced me over the years. They include Dave Olesen, John McPhee, Aldo Leopold, Richard K. Nelson, Michael Furtman, Barton Sutter, Barry Lopez, Colin Fletcher, and many more. In ways most of them don't know, they have helped shape my writing and my view of the natural world.

Finally, my thanks to Don Tubesing, Casey McGee, and all the others at Pfeifer-Hamilton for their care and counsel in originally putting these pieces together in book form.

Sam Cook
Duluth, Minnesota

Contents

Rhythms of the Land

Crustwalking

The Ojibway have a name for it: *Onabani-gisiss.*

Moon of the crust on the snow. It's the full moon of March.

What you want to do is get up early. Not duck-hunting early, but early enough that the sun hasn't begun to work on the snow.

Awaiting you, early in the morning in the middle of March, is some of the best traveling of the year.

Crustwalking.

What has happened is that recent warm spells melted the top few inches of snow. Softened it. Settled it. And now, on below-freezing mornings, that snow is set up into a crust so firm you can walk anywhere on it.

At first, it's almost difficult to leave familiar trails behind. They, too, are set up and firm for walking. But to

truly appreciate crustwalking, you have to leave the beaten
path and wander—aimlessly—through the woods.

I did some crustwalking one morning this week. It was a
15-degree morning, and the crust was impeccable.

I lit out up a hill. The first sensation of crustwalking is
almost one of giddiness. It feels so good to be moving so easily, on top, after a winter of shuffling or mooshing or plunging along. The sunlight didn't hurt the mood either.

A friend of mine who had been crustwalking a couple of
days earlier said he felt almost as if he were floating. There is
the undeniable sense of being above something, on top, almost cheating.

The snow flows along over the contour of whatever is below—the smooth forest floor, rocks, the occasional deadfall
tree. But up on top, all is smooth and white and firm. It's as if
you were walking on petrified frosting. It feels good, too. The
snow is neither glazed nor slick underfoot. The top quarter-
inch of snow crystals crunches underfoot. The way it feels, you
could be walking on a crumbled layer of malted milk balls.

I walked down the hill and crossed a ski trail, resisting the
urge to follow it. I moved into some alder lowlands pocked
with deer tracks.

As pure as the walking was, the snow was not pristine. It
was littered with pieces of bark, sprigs of pine boughs, tufts
of lichen, bleached maple leaves, and tatters of birchbark. All
of these provided more evidence of the coming season of
warmth. Being organic matter—and simply being darker than
the snow around them—these bits and pieces were soaking
up the sun's warmth faster than the surrounding whiteness.
As a result, they were recessed into the snow in perfect leaf-
shaped and bark-shaped and lichen-shaped receptacles.

The same goes for the deer droppings, of which there
were plenty.

At first, I thought crustwalking was almost as good as summer hiking. Then I thought again. It might be better. It's certainly less restrictive. In summer, when the undergrowth is lush and thick, you can't walk unfettered through the woods. Except in open pine stands, you're bound to stay on trails. Now, on top, with only the occasional bare branch to push out of the way, you can go anywhere.

And of course, mosquitoes are no problem.

Crustwalking is sort of like daydreaming on your feet. You let your eyes lead the way. You can skirt the far shore of the beaver pond you never ventured near in open-water season. You see a big white pine you want to check out? Change course. Go look up its trunk. You see a patch of feathers off to one side? Angle over there. Looks like a grouse died.

The one thing you're not likely to see while crustwalking is another crustwalker. Because you're not on a trail, the chances of encountering someone else are slim. I came across beaver tracks, dog tracks, grouse tracks, and deer tracks. But I saw only one set of crustwalker tracks. When I came across them, I made sure to go in a different direction than the tracks did. It seemed to be in keeping with the spirit of crustwalking.

It was a great morning's walk. I could think of possibly one better kind of walk—crustwalking at night under a good moon.

The moon of the crust on the snow.

Onabani-gisiss.

Return to the Brule

I know I'm there when I see the bald eagle circling overhead.

If the time is late March and you're traveling a northwestern Wisconsin back road and there's an eagle in the sky, chances are you're near the Brule River.

The truck rumbles along the road, headed for Stone's Bridge, where I'll put a canoe on the Brule on this March morning. One bend past the eagle, I'm there. I get out and stand in the parking lot for a few moments, smelling the air, letting the hurry go out of me.

Coming back to the Brule in March is something of a ritual. It's a passage of sorts, like coming home after being gone a long time.

I am alone today. I called a couple of people to see if they wanted to come with me, but they couldn't. I would have enjoyed their company, but this is fine. I will take my time, poking along silently.

The river is low. It is so clear it seems to be a pane of glass through which I can see the silty bottom, rocks, and the swaying aquatic growth.

The canoe rides on the current like a piece of straw. I kneel amidships. The canoe responds to every push and twist of the paddle.

Putting a paddle blade in the water after a long, white winter in the North is like a sigh that comes flowing out from deep inside you. Several layers of winter come sliding off your shoulders, and you shed the heaviness of those dark months like old skin.

The sun is out. My thermometer calibrates the air temperature at 44, the water at 39. I point the canoe toward Lake Superior and begin the quiet downstream odyssey.

Do not get the idea that spring is bursting out all over. Snow still lies in the woods. Shelf ice clings to the banks, especially on the shady south shore. Feathery skim ice—from last night—extends from the shelf ice.

On the way over, I noticed that both the Amnicon and Middle Rivers were still locked in ice and snow. But the Brule, fed by numerous springs along its length, nearly always opens sooner than the rest.

The eagles know that.

I will paddle several miles of the river without hearing or seeing a single human. Semitrailers will downshift along Wisconsin Highway 27 where it follows the river near Big Lake, and a propane truck will lumber into the Ordway Estate at Cedar Island. But beyond that, the sounds will be natural.

Crows call in the distance. A gray jay swoops down to the river and cocks his round head at me. Suddenly, I think I hear a deer walking at the edge of the river behind me. But, no. It's only my lazy wake lapping at the underside of some shelf ice. Glup, glup, glup.

All of the bends are like old friends. Familiar cedars hang low and must be skirted. Familiar rocks rear their bald heads above the river's surface.

I have seen, what—a dozen spring seasons come to this river? I wonder, ducking under a cedar, how many springs these old trees must have seen. How many mergansers have returned to cruise beneath them in courting plumage? How many deer have lapped water near their smooth trunks? How many muskrats have breast-stroked in the cedar shadows like wet gloves squeezing themselves across the riverbed?

These cedars make a paddler feel like a little boy against the stretch of time.

A blue jay goes to clamoring in the forest. As if for a comparison of decibel levels, a pileated woodpecker launches into his ascending yammer. Farther along comes the soft "Hey, Petey" call of a chickadee.

I don't know how far I'll paddle. It could be four miles. It could be six or eight. This is not the kind of paddle you measure in miles, or even hours. Time seems such a relative commodity out here. The sun in the southeast for a time, then due south, then behind you somewhere in the southwest. The day, like the river beneath the canoe, slides by.

I have forgotten how good it can be to spend time alone in a canoe. I half-figure I'll come upon some cabin dweller replacing a shingle on a boathouse or putting new screens on a porch. I see us, in my mind, talking for a few minutes about the river and the day and the season.

But I see no one, and that's fine. I'm free to concentrate on the silence and the sunshine, on the flittings and fleeings along the shores, on the movement of the canoe.

Deer are everywhere in the open woods. One, two of them at river left, on a broad hillside. Three, four, five, six farther along. I doubt I would see them if they remained still, but they hightail it away from the river. I see the brown shapes scattering among the trees and the white tails tossing.

The farther I move downriver, the more wildlife I see. Two deer, river left. A pair of mallards erupting into flight at Cedar Island. Seven deer, river left. One, river right. Two more on the right.

I stop and find a place to boil a pot of tea. Lunch is what I threw together too fast at home—peanut butter and jelly sandwich, cheese, an orange, a few caramels.

At Lucius Lake, a bulge in the Brule, sentinel eagles glare down at me from the two nests there. One eagle is near the upstream nest. Two are near the downstream nest. One of them, after a time, drops from his branch and swoops to another white pine farther downriver. He wants to keep an eye on me, maybe.

At a wide spot a few bends below Lucius Lake, the movement of the canoe freezes two deer on the bank. They flick ears and try to get a fix on me. That's when the eight mallards flush, quacking with indignation. Only then do the four Canada geese take flight, ca-ronking their way around a bend.

Then I see why. The geese are joining maybe twenty more that are loafing on a lobe of skim ice in the bay. They waddle and preen and eye me warily. Finally, they can tolerate no more, and they run themselves across the ice until they're airborne.

They seem almost too large for the river. Their black wings seem to touch trees on both sides as they swing downstream and gain altitude. Their honking, always beautiful, is even more resonant in this deep valley.

I sit in the canoe for a long time in the silence the geese leave behind them, pondering on those big birds, the wonder of migration, and my good fortune.

I see a few steelhead—not as many as I hoped to see—on their spawning grounds between Lucius Lake and the Highway B bridge. They are dark shadows zinging away from the canoe. Big dark shadows. They will work themselves ragged over the next few weeks making another crop of steelhead— the wild rainbow trout that eventually move down to Lake Superior.

At the takeout, I stash the canoe and hop on my bicycle. Half an hour later, I'm back with the truck. I load the canoe and toss the pack and paddles into the vehicle.

When I pull out from the roadside to leave, my eyes catch movement in the sky over the river.

Two eagles.

I suppose a person could consider that merely coincidence. But I don't.

Skydance

The woodcock appeared out of the west, a twitter of wings against low-slung clouds. He was right on time.

It was dusk on an evening in May. The light had faded to the point that when we saw the bird on the ground, we weren't sure for a moment whether we were seeing the bird or a clod of dirt.

The two of us had been there for at least half an hour, waiting for the light to get right. When you go out to watch the woodcock's sky dance, you don't want to miss the opening act.

Nearly every evening from mid-April to mid-May in the North Country, male woodcock appear in clearings and roadways to perform their act of courtship. Presumably the female of the species is lurking someplace where she can appreciate the show, although I have never seen or heard anything but males.

The woodcock is something of a weird bird, having been dealt an upside-down brain, a build something like Charles Kuralt, and a bill almost three inches long. The woodcock uses the bill to probe the earth for worms.

We have watched the sky dance in other years, but we keep coming back for more. Like the calling of frogs—another ritual of courtship—the woodcock's sky dance is an event worth experiencing each spring.

The woodcock landed in an open grassy area where he must have felt he could be observed by any available females. My wife and I were sitting on the ground next to some brush, facing west. It is essential, when watching the sky dance, to face west so you can see the bird against the fading light of the day.

Almost immediately upon landing, the woodcock began uttering his characteristic nasal peent. He peented every two or three seconds for probably a couple of minutes. Then he was gone.

The sky dance had begun. The bird whiffled upward, making an intermittent whistling sound. Birding guides say the bird makes this sound with its wings. The woodcock rose until he was lost in the waning light.

The next thing you hear is what one birding book calls a "bubbling warble." What it sounds like is some very serious kissing. That's your signal the bird is on his way down, although we could always hear the warbling long before we pick up the flight of the bird.

Suddenly, the bird was down again, ready for more peenting. A woodcock nearly always lands precisely at the spot from which he left, and if you're quick you can move closer to the spot while he's in the air.

We did, getting to within ten steps of the peenting hotspot. I counted while the woodcock peented. One series lasted only twelve peents, and he was airborne again. Another one, thirty-two peents. Another, fifty-two.

Between peents, we could hear something we had never noticed in other sky dances—a chortle. It sounded like a swallowed hiccup, and it continued throughout the peenting.

While a woodcock peents, he carries his roundish head cocked at the ground. He appears to waddle around on his toothpick-thin legs, like a man trying to locate some change he has lost on the ground.

Unlike other woodcock we have watched, this one alternated between two landing pads. We guessed he had a couple of ladies on the line.

The show lasted precisely forty-five minutes, until the woodcock was all peented out or until he figured it was too dark to show his stuff.

The performance ended with no flourish. The woodcock, in mid-peent, must have just walked into the woods for the night.

Gotta get some rest, you know. Courtship is stressful.

Frogsong

The frogs began calling in the little pond behind our home on April 27. That's the latest they've begun since we've lived there, but it was worth the wait.

It always is.

The wood frogs started first, muttering in their quacklike style. As usual, they had the pond to themselves for only a couple of days before the audacious peepers cut loose. Now, they both call every night, nearly all night, and even on some afternoons when the humidity is running high.

I suppose if we lived on a lake, we would define spring by the wail of the first loon. But we don't, so we trust the frogs to keep us posted.

They've begun calling at our place as early as April 17 in some years. We know because we write the dates on our calendar each year, carrying forward our first-frog records from all previous years.

As with those who welcome martins or geese or swallows, a part of our world is brightened each April by the love-inspired baying of frogs.

Some nights, walking the dog from one pool of frogs to another in our neighborhood, I stop and listen to this crescendo of croaking. I'm always astounded by the unbridled passion with which these tiny amphibians sing. And they do it all night, every night, for a month or more each spring. Sure, the survival of the species is at stake, but you can't help but admire that kind of persistence.

Standing there with the dog in the dark, I want to shout, "Yes! Sing it boys!"

Once the peepers start calling, they dominate any pond. They shriek, "Deep! Knee-deep! Deep! Deep! Knee-deep!" They sound like crickets on steroids. Their calls overlap each other until it is almost a single continuous note that reverberates among the leafless trees.

The wood frogs provide a percussion of sorts beneath the din of the peepers. If peepers and wood frogs sang the "Little Drummer Boy" at Christmas, the wood frogs would be stuck singing all the "pa-rump-a-pum-pums."

I wish our bedroom faced the little pond, so I could throw our windows open at night and drift off to sleep to that music. But I do the next-best thing.

Once almost every spring, I pitch a tent in the backyard and spend a night with the frogs. Last Saturday, I knew it was the night. The air was cool and damp, and frogsong seemed to permeate the woods.

By the light of a headlamp, I pitched the small tent and threw a sleeping bag inside. As soon as I crawled into the down envelope, I heard something besides frogs: a gentle tapping on the tent. Rain.

I lay there immersed in the night and the rain and the singing. It was as if the whole world were liquid. The sky and the pond had become one. Half in the pool below and half in the saturated world above, the frogs called with newfound inspiration. Rainy nights always bring on the best calling.

I came half-awake several times during the night. Always, the music from the pond came wafting through the tent to wash over me. I'd listen for a moment then drift back into frogsleep.

Going Solo

Sometimes, you know you are going to have to get away for a while, by yourself, and do almost nothing. You feel it coming on. The need builds for months or weeks or even days, and you know you must go.

To the cabin.

To the lake.

Or just to someplace you know in the woods.

Maybe you'll take a fishing rod. Maybe you'll take the dog. Maybe you'll take a book.

None of that matters much. Each person has his or her own idea of what's essential for this kind of steal-away. The important thing is that you don't take too much of anything. You want to keep this simple if it is going to work.

I remember a friend saying, late in the summer a couple of years ago, that he was going to the canoe country. Alone.

He had been hitting it too hard and for too long at work, he said. He could feel the pressure accumulating. But he had his window of opportunity, and he was going.

"I'm going to take some wild rice, and I'm going to catch some fish," he said. "If I don't catch fish, I'll just eat rice."

I liked the simplicity of his plan. Granted, those meals were going to be a lot better if he caught a walleye or two, but this friend almost always catches fish. I wasn't concerned about him going hungry.

Although he never checked in after his trip to say how he had gotten along, I didn't expect him to. Barring a big storm or a close encounter with a moose, the trip was probably uneventful. You can pretty easily figure what a person would do out there.

Fish a little. Lie around. Read. Gather some firewood. Skinny-dip. Lie around. Contemplate old pines and young insects. Study some clouds. Lie around. Listen to the water greeting a ledge of granite. Take a nap. Build a fire. Watch it slowly die.

That would be about it. That is mostly what a person does on a getaway like that. What's equally important is what a mind does. And what it does not do.

As you idle away at small tasks around the cabin, lie on a rock in the canoe country, mosey down some quiet trail in the woods, your mind is free to drift where it will. To think about things that matter a lot. To think about things that matter very little.

Somehow, it is much easier to think objectively about life, marriage, children, goals, and dreams when you're focusing mostly on sky, soil, rock, trees, and water.

Gordon MacQuarrie, who grew up in Superior and went on to a career as an outdoor editor for the *Milwaukee Journal*, understood the need for these times alone. In his essay "Nothing To Do For Three Weeks," MacQuarrie writes, "There is much to be said in behalf of the solitary way of fishing and hunting. It lets people get acquainted with themselves."

Which is, after all, mostly what we're after. Stripping away all of the excess. Getting down to the essentials of life. Taking with you only the luxury of time.

You will know when the time is right. When you have to make your move. When you have to go to where your soul and your mind can roam free for a while.

There is only one way to do it.

Alone.

The Sound of Rain

Stirring to consciousness in the middle of the night, I was aware that rain had begun to fall. Lying in my sleeping bag, snug in the tent, I stayed awake for a few moments listening.

There are plenty of good sounds in the woods—wind in the pine boughs, small waves licking a spit of rock, loons riding the night sky. But the tapping of rain on a good tent is as therapeutic a sound as you can come by in the back country.

A good tent. That's an essential ingredient to the experience.

If you can lie there, reasonably sure that the rain will remain on the outside of the tent, you can drift in and out of sleep blissfully.

It hasn't always been that way in my camping life. I remember as a kid sleeping in canvas tents, making sure not to touch the canvas during a hard rain. The theory was that by touching the canvas, you would somehow draw the moisture through to the inside of the tent. A small drip would become a rivulet, which would eventually form a pool on the tent floor, if not on your sleeping bag.

I don't recall this ever happening, but I lived in moderate fear of Touching the Canvas for a good part of my childhood.

In my early days of camping on my own, we had an A-frame poplin tent. Better than canvas, but still nothing like today's nylon tent-and-fly combinations. One night, in a horrendous thunderstorm on Little Crab Lake in the canoe country north of Ely, we lay there in the dark. We pulled a small tarp over us and managed to pass the night in a mostly dry condition.

The more vivid memory of that night is the aroma of the dog we had then, Dave, who was deathly afraid of thunder and lightning. We had let him into the tent wet, and he spent the night lying between us, whimpering. I think he was under the tarp, too.

Even after we had graduated to a state-of-the-art nylon tent, we found ways to ensure adventure during a rain. I remember a night camped on an island in Kawnipi Lake in Ontario's Quetico Provincial Park. It was one of those campsites that have been used hard over the years, and its soil, what there was left of it, had been compacted to something resembling concrete.

We happened to pitch our tent over a small depression in the hardpan soil. Then the rains came. But we weren't worried. We had a good tent. And we had a waterproof tarp beneath it for extra protection.

Trouble was, the rain ran from the hardpan ground over the *top* of the tarp beneath our tent. It wasn't long before we were sleeping, essentially, on a waterbed. There must have been an inch or two of water pooled between that tarp and our tent floor. Inside the tent, we were almost floating. We spent the rest of the night trying to find any solid ground under us, most of which was along one edge of the tent. The two of us—Phyllis and I—scrunched along that high ground and slept fitfully until morning.

But we've ridden out some good rains, too. We spent most of an evening on Trant Lake in the Quetico watching massive thunderheads build in the west. Not long after we had gone to bed, the skies unleashed. It was as if someone had built a scaffolding around our tent and about twenty people were standing up there dumping buckets on us.

That tent held like a champ. Do you know how satisfying it is to lie in that kind of downpour dry and snug? It is possibly the apex of self-sufficiency. Traveling light. Getting by. Staying dry.

We lay awake until we were sure there would be no trickles from the corners, and as the hard rain eased into a random patter of drops, we drifted off into slumber.

Another rain found us camped on a sand spit at the confluence of the Gods and Hayes Rivers in northern Manitoba. After 200 miles on the Gods River and a string of Manitoba lakes, we were only a two-day paddle from Hudson Bay. The six of us had planned to rise early and catch the quick current of the river on its way to York Factory, a historic Hudson Bay Company trading post near the bay.

In a quick tent-to-tent conference in the early-morning hours, we called off any thoughts of paddling at sunrise. Then we dropped back into sleep with the rain drumming over our heads. We had been on the trail for almost three weeks. We had established a simple rhythm to each day— breaking camp, eating, paddling, making camp, sleeping.

And now, for a change, we were allotted a couple of extra hours of delicious rest.

I have awakened many mornings since then, pressed to get up and get to work, and longed for the luxury of that morning.

On the river.

In a tent.

In the rain.

The Dawning of Autumn

The sun will be rising in fifteen minutes, and I am ready for it. I have come here alone, high on the ridge overlooking Lake Superior, to wait for the sun.

The northeastern sky over the lake is brushed with clouds that resemble Nike swoosh stripes in fuchsia. Directly above the place where I think the sun will rise, a streak of low clouds is tinged peach and orange. For a moment on this October morning, the colors in the sky have subdued the fall colors on the hillside below.

The woods and the weekends have been brilliant lately, but I have been moving through them too fast. I need this morning, this moment, to finally sit still and steep myself in the season. I choose a piece of Skyline Parkway not far from Hawk Ridge.

I opt to not even leave the car. This has been the coldest morning of fall so far. Thirty-three degrees. I'm happy to be ensconced in this artificial warmth. I have a 180-degree view of Duluth and Lake Superior and the distant Wisconsin shoreline. The windows are clean.

This is always a bittersweet time of year for me. I love fall and everything it represents—hunting of all kinds, cross-country races on rolling golf courses, the harvest from the garden, the smell of the woods. But I cannot deny that I'll miss open water, the night-dancing of wind in the oak leaves outside my bedroom window, and the patterns of shade on the green grass.

Walking the dog after dark the other night, I glimpsed winter: two trees, leafless and naked against the night sky, their branches reaching for the sky like withered tentacles. The night was warm, but for just a moment I was jerked into January. Those branches looked cold and hard and lonely. I could envision them traced with fresh snow. I could hear a cold wind sifting through them.

All the more reason to be on this ridge Friday morning. I sit in the car and watch the sky change by the moment. The color leaches out of the swoosh stripes. The light intensifies on the clouds just over the sun-rising place.

Then, a single point of radiance on the dark Wisconsin shoreline. A laser tip of orange. A neon speck.

Not an arc. Not a segment of a sphere. Not a spilling over of color.

It is the day's initial sunbeam, piercing its way through— what, a stand of white pines in Wisconsin? But only for a second. Then the entire form of the sun appears, emerges, climbs as if on some electronic track.

And for these seconds after sunrise, I am reminded again that the planet spins. That our scurrying about on what seems to be unmoving rock and water is just an illusion. It's we who are hardly moving, while the planet itself is engaged in constant rotation.

Now the sun is too bright to look at any longer. I concentrate instead on a long shaft of orange lying on a placid Lake Superior. Yesterday, in the wind and the whitecaps, that beam would have been shattered into a million fragments. Today it looks like the single, rich stroke from a giant brush.

I can take it no longer. I have to get outside. The light has reached a desk of basalt on the hillside behind me, and I have to go there, sit, feel the substance of the rock beneath me, touch the lichen, smell the rotting fallen leaves around me.

School buses and vans rumble in the city far below. The sunlight burnishes the tips of aspen below and leaves dark shadows in the low spots. Not far away, both the leaves and the stems of a red osier dogwood glow blood-red. The needles of a nearby Scotch pine appear to ignite.

I imagine this same rock several months from now, when March sunrises have finally melted the snow from it again, when its bare surface signals the coming of another season of plenty.

It has been a good summer.

Being in the Woods

The spot would have to be right. It would have to be catching the sun's afternoon rays, and it would have to be partway up a gentle rise. The ideal spot would offer a view of sorts—a clearing in the forest, maybe, or a small pothole.

I walked along a trail I knew, past dried ferns the color of chocolate.

I knew what I wanted to do when I found the spot. I wanted to sit, quietly, and become part of the woods.

Grouse hunting has given me ample time to be in the woods, but when you are grouse hunting, you are moving. You are moving and listening and alert, ready to bring up your shotgun at the first sound of pounding wings.

This time, I didn't want to be a hunter. I merely wanted to be there, to see what I might see and hear what there was to hear.

I went for the same reason that someone else might cut out of work early on an October afternoon and head for the cabin. To make some wood. To repair the eaves. To clean a woodstove chimney. Those would be the stated reasons, anyway.

But I suspect the cabin owner would want as much simply to be alone, to notice the flittings of the chickadees, to appreciate the color of the moss on an old stump, or to be aware that the sky no longer looks like a summer sky.

I was talking the other day to a man who said this was his favorite time of the year. He may have been a hunter, but he didn't say so. What he said was that he loves to be in the woods. That is exactly how he said it—"to be in the woods."

I'm sure bow hunters must hunt deer for some of the same reasons. Yes, there are the deer, but I know too many bow hunters who pass up shots early in the season to believe that shooting a deer is their driving force for being in the woods.

They are perhaps the quintessential woods sitters, the bow hunters. They know how to become part of the woods—to be silent, to be still, to watch. I was visiting with a bow hunter the other day. He talked about going to his deer stand and spending the first half-hour "letting the woods settle down."

He was talking about becoming part of the country—letting the blue jays that betrayed his arrival move on, letting the birds begin to move naturally again, letting the collective countryside, in effect, forget he was there.

I was thinking those kinds of thoughts when I saw a place. It was near a tiny water hole where I had once missed a drake mallard I surprised. The pothole was dry now, but there was mud where it used to be, and deer tracks pocked the mud.

A popple just up a small ridge from the pond opening seemed to offer a suitable backrest. I sat down, pruned some brush, and looked around. I could feel sun on my face. A whisper of a breeze breathed past me, coming from the east.

This was the spot.

Like a bowless bow hunter, I sat. I watched grass and leaves and the play of light on the naked popples. I didn't know what I might see. I hoped for a deer.

A spider the color of old straw crawled up on my pant legs and made himself at home. He was either missing one of his eight legs or dragging one. I couldn't tell.

I felt the wind on my left cheek. It was too light to make sound in the trees, at least in the leafless trees of October. But dead strands of grass hanging from still-green shoots swung in the air's current.

I couldn't help noticing, sitting there, the imperfection of the woods. An aspen had been lopped off at half-mast. Another one grew straight for fifteen feet, then abruptly took a right turn before continuing skyward. Other trees were bent. Some, having died as adolescents, lay across others in abbreviated falls to the forest floor.

What we think of as the woods—a living, vital place—is in truth a collection of the pretty and not so pretty, the healthy and unhealthy, the living and the dead. Not everything makes it out here. Not everything that makes it makes it easily.

It's impossible to sit on the flank of a knoll and not ponder the forces that bring about all of this imperfection. A wet, heavy snow. A spring ice storm. A series of wet years or a series of dry ones. Army worms. Spruce budworms. A fire. Absence of fire.

We in our civilized world are accustomed to direct cause and effect, neat closure on the processes we initiate. We spray our lawns; weeds die. A birch dies; we have it cut up and hauled off. A branch falls on our grass; we toss it in the alley.

It doesn't work that way in the woods. For a reason. For lots of reasons, some probably too complex for us to understand.

But you can get at them, or at least ponder them, sitting in the woods on a October afternoon.

Mysteries on the Wing

The immediate danger in opening the truck doors was that they might be peeled backward on their hinges by the wind.

The wind was screaming out of the northwest on a late October afternoon in western Minnesota. Rain had been falling since midday, and now, an hour before dusk, every wet projectile stabbed our camouflage parkas.

Four of us, and two Labrador retrievers, hustled from the trucks down a trail to the marsh.

It was a raw, nasty, horrible, beautiful evening to hunt ducks.

The weather service had called it. Winds building to 40 m.p.h. by evening. Temperatures plummeting overnight. For nearly a month, duck season had been warm and pleasant and unducky. No storms to move many ducks south. No winds for those handsome creatures to ride across the night skies. No freezing temperatures to begin locking up those northern marshes.

Now it appeared this was the night.

Before we even had a chance to discuss who would hunt where, a turbulence of gadwalls appeared above us. The wind swallowed the sound of our gunshots, and two gadwalls fell. Somehow the dogs saw them and plunged into the water to retrieve them.

Quickly, we walked out on a spit of land that bisected the shallow wetland. Splitting into two pairs, we took up positions standing in head-high cattails, one dog with each set of hunters.

I have never hunted ducks on a wilder evening. Looking into the wind was an exercise in sheer suffering. The driven rain made it feel as if someone were throwing rice at our faces. Except that rice doesn't drip slowly down your neck and sleeves.

Water ran down our gun barrels. Wind lashed the cattails. The dog hunkered down with her rear end just off the saturated muck. Water matted her fur and trickled down her back. She shivered. Was it cold or anticipation?

Light was already being sucked from what little the day had parceled out. The ceiling was low. Blackbirds, traveling in packs, shot over the marsh with astonishing speed. We could have caught them with a landing net.

From every direction, ducks materialized out of the bleak beyond. Green-winged teal dipped and wheeled over the spit of land. Mallards wrestled with the wind, approaching from the south.

Forgotten were all of those bluebird days when the ducks flew high or not at all. Gone were all the memories of silent dawns when not a breath of breeze rippled the marshes.

Ducks were over us almost all the time. Some arrived and left before we could shoulder our guns. We passed shots on southbound ducks, knowing that even if we managed to hit one, the wind would carry it far beyond the range of our retrievers.

We shot some ducks. Our partners shot some ducks. Many, many more settled into the cattails beyond gun range.

We shot until what we knew, according to the hunting regulations, and our watches, to be sunset. Then we stopped.

That's when the ducks really began to pour in.

We stood there on the spit in plain view, dogs standing at our sides. There was no way anyone who loved ducks and duck hunting could have left.

We watched them pile into that little marsh on all sides of us. They came without caution, dropped out of the sky, seeking shelter from the storm.

We would turn to walk out and stop again to stare. We have all heard about the Grand Passages of years past, continent-wide movements of waterfowl sweeping down from the north.

If this wasn't a Grand Passage, it was at least a grand evening. These ducks were part of all the wild North, part of the great Canadian prairies. Standing there for a few moments on that windswept finger of land, we somehow shared in all they represented. The struggle for new life in the spring. The fullness of life on those endless summer days. And now, the mystery of migration.

We stood there until darkness was almost complete, then snugged our hoods and marched into the wind.

Superior Storm

For thirty-six hours, the east wind had been howling across Lake Superior. Now, at midday, it showed no signs of abating.

At Duluth's Canal Park, metal signs shimmied in the wind. Sheets of spray ripped across the parking lot in horizontal streaks. Light posts quivered.

But the hunched figures who scurried about hadn't come to see what was happening on land. They had come to witness the fury and tumult of the world's largest expanse of fresh water.

It was a fine show.

I left my car and forced myself into the wind, out to the lakeshore. I didn't make it. I stopped short, huddling behind a decorative cluster of timbers.

The driven rain stung my unsheltered face. Waves hammered desk-sized boulders twenty feet ahead of me. Spumes

of spray shot for the sky but were whipped across the boardwalk at eye level.

Suddenly, outside the tunnel of my parka hood, I noticed
a man standing nearby.

"Not bad," I said.

"Not bad," he said, smiling a wet smile.

"You from here?" he asked.

"Yeah. You?" I asked.

"Yeah," he said. "But you still have to come down and
see it."

Which is to say for us that living in Duluth, it would
have been easy to sit up on the hillside and know what a 50-
knot wind would be doing to the lake. But sometimes, simply knowing it is not enough. You have to come down, park
the car, get out, get stung by those tracer-bullet raindrops,
and feel it.

Everywhere, there were others like us, scampering through
puddles, challenging the spray, snapping photos.

It was difficult to face the relentless wind and that sting-
ing rain for long, but you had to. You had to see those waves.
What were they—eight, ten, twelve feet? How do you measure waves like that? And how do you describe the feeling
inside you when you watch one gathering itself, heaving upward, now beginning to curl, now spilling like water rushing
over a dam as wide as a football field? And that was just one
of them. They were stacked up out there—seething, surging,
frothing—almost to the horizon.

When my jeans were soaked, I ran to the Marine Museum and sought shelter. At least thirty people were lined
up around the curved windows of the second floor. Moms
and kids. Dads and kids. Men in suits. A man with a cellu-
lar phone on his hip. College kids. Old men, alone. Boy-
friends and girlfriends.

On a television monitor, terse phrases tried to portray what we seeing outside.

"Temperature: Mid-30s. Wind: East, 35 to 45 knots, gusts to 50 knots. Waves: 9 to 12 feet, 12 to 16 feet."

For the record, 50 knots is $57^{1}/_{2}$ miles per hour.

Then the screen changed. A new heading came up.

"Today's Vessel Traffic," it said.

And below it, three almost eerie words: "No known vessels."

From the railing, from our own ship's pilothouse, we all stood and watched the waves roll down through the Duluth Ship Canal. From here, one could put them in some kind of perspective. They were massive.

It is ten feet from normal water level to the top of the pier walls, a museum attendant said. Many of the waves made the trip kissing the very top of the concrete walls all the way. A lot of them came spilling over the top, and the walkways were always awash in the turbid water.

And then a wave would come that made the others look small. It would hump itself up, up and over the pier wall, shouldering its way along the wall, smacking light posts, racing along the canal—a frightening, exhilarating thing to see.

A man from of Duluth had been there for an hour and a half.

"You've gotta sit and wait and wait for one good one," he said. "I saw one that was six feet over the pier wall. But just one."

These weren't walls of water. They were entire rooms of water, gymnasiums full of water. There was a sense of mass and weight to them that was beyond anything we usually associate with waves.

"Can you imagine being out there in those waves?" I asked the man.

"Oh, God," was all he said.

I couldn't resist one more pass by the lake when I left. I was out in the debris zone, with the rocks that had been tossed across the boardwalk, when I looked up and saw a gull working its way along the shore—flying—wrestling with the wind, yes, but holding its own, searching the waves.

I couldn't imagine a gull being that hungry. Or that tough.

Cutting Fat

A hardness falls upon the land.

November.

The big chill is upon us, tightening the land the way a cold wind tightens an exposed cheek. All of the softness is gone now. The suppleness of leaves. The vitality of grass. The spirit of songbirds.

A friend of mine went paddling a couple of weekends ago. He was struck by the silence in the woods. The nearly total silence.

Water was still liquid then, but now that, too, is changing. As the land tightens, constricts, so does the water. The last shred of elasticity in the country, sapped by November.

And the light, once yellow-gold, now low and lean, almost pure white. Winter light. Pastel at dawn maybe. Streaked with rose at dusk, maybe, beneath a bank of cloud. But by day, the light is thin and clear. November light. December light. Light without heat.

We have known this was coming, felt it in our bones, felt the firming of the earth beneath our boot soles. First, it was simply the absence of lushness. Then the crisping of ferns and grasses. Now this.

Hardness. A world without give.

We have scurried against this tightening of the land. Hauled in hoses. Swaddled shrubs. Laid in two-gallon supplies of snowblower gas.

Retrieved lawn chairs, stacked wood, caulked cracks, filled bird feeders, found mittens, sealed doors, lined up boots, pulled up carrots, stowed canoes, checked antifreeze, canned beets, bagged leaves, parked mowers, readied shovels, mounted plow blades, drained lower units, stashed grills.

And in doing so, tightened our lives. Cut out the fat. Simplified. Leaned down.

In some inexplicable northern way, we enjoyed it. There's a clean kind of satisfaction to all of this battening down, all this putting away, all of this getting ready.

It looks good, the bare lay of the ground, the absence of excess around the home place.

It has come down to this now. Efficiency. It will be important not to expend extra energy. Winter will require enough from us as it is. We must keep our lives simple, eliminate the wide turns, the extra steps, the possibility of complication.

I have lived where none of this mattered, or mattered so much less, as to be not a factor in life. I would miss it now, having known this way. Would miss the cold, the dark, the hardship. Would miss the silence of snow. Would miss the intricacy of ice.

Life would be easier without all of that. Less demanding. More comfortable. I may live that way someday. Might find the time is right for it. But would always miss this part. The part that reminds us that we are not in charge here. That we can be humbled, even stopped dead in our tracks once in a while.

Like the animals, we'd better be ready.

We hunker down now. And wait.

The hardness is upon us.

November.

Black Ice

Early in the week, the word came down.

Black ice.

Black ice on the St. Louis River. Great skating. Smooth, black ice. Miles of it.

You don't take black ice for granted. You take it today, because tomorrow it might be gone. An inch of snow, and the game is over. For the year. Maybe for two, three years.

I heard about it Monday morning. Black ice on the river. Just before sundown, we were there. Two of us.

We put in on one of those deep Wisconsin bays that reaches into the city of Superior like so many fingers. We crunched across some rotten yellow ice near the shore, where overflow from a spring was trying to freeze. We skated across the bay ice—gray, ordinary stuff.

And then we hit it.

Black ice.

As far as you could see toward the setting sun or the rising moon. Smooth, black ice.

The name is misleading. Black ice isn't black. It is, in fact, almost perfectly clear. It is the dark water, the mysterious depths beneath it, that makes it look black.

If you haven't skated black ice before, your first encounter with it is unnerving. It is so clear you cannot convince yourself of its reliability.

I got down on my knees and peered into it. I wanted reassurance. I knew people had been skating on it all weekend, up and down the river. But I had to inspect it, check it out for myself.

We scrutinized a crack, where we could gauge the thickness of the ice. Four inches, we figured. Most people consider that plenty of ice for safe travel on foot.

My friend began gobbling up huge bites of ice in clean, fast strides straight at the sunset.

"You just have to put it out of your mind and trust," he yelled over a shoulder.

With that, we were off, skimming across the transparent skin of hard water. Isolated patches of windswept snow, like albino amoebas, blotted the ice in places. But mostly it was ice. Black ice with tiny gray bubbles. Black ice with cracks that looked like horizontal lightning. Black ice that seemed not to be ice at all.

The impression isn't that you're traveling over something. It is, instead, as if you are floating. You are floating somewhere beneath the sky and somewhere above this liquid medium that you know, intellectually, is below you. You don't believe that what you are doing is possible. It is cheating, somehow, or maybe some kind of out-of-body experience.

And the beauty of it is that you could go forever. In fact, you feel as if you must go forever. To stop would shatter the illusion that all of this is happening, that you are floating between the sky and the water.

Up ahead, my partner was flying down the single sunbeam on the ice, legs pumping, arms swinging, skates singing. He was a rhythmic collection of black appendages backlit by a tongue of fire on the ice.

Finally, we peeled off from the tangerine runway and began probing the finger bays of rural Superior. We skimmed across the jumbled transition ice, onto the gray ice, onto black ice frosted by a feathering of snow. Over fox tracks and raccoon tracks and ice-fisherman tracks. Into the dusky recesses.

Deep in those bays, we stopped and listened—listened to the quiet and the sound of ourselves breathing. Once, when my partner skated off, I put my ear to the ice and listened to the sound he made. Each crisp stride was made up of a push-off and glide. It sounded like someone chewing crackers.

Daylight gave way to dusk. The moon, almost full, rose over Lake Superior, over Ontario, over Quebec and Labrador. High clouds moved in from the northwest. They looked like shark's gills.

As we had skated into the sunset, we now made for black ice and skated into the moonrise. It was, if anything, more magical.

A beam of quicksilver on the ice. Duluth, lighting up, over one shoulder. The silent woods of Wisconsin over the other.

Wind on your face. Wings on your feet. Moonshadows coming on.

Speed and light and magic.

Black ice on the river.

Family Ties

Slim Chance

We stood there on the shore of Slim Lake, watching the canoe out on the water. Our canoe. With no one aboard.

Clearly, this was about to become the most memorable
event of a weekend outing in the Boundary Waters Canoe
Area Wilderness for my son, Grant, 5, and me.

It had happened without so much as a sound. We had
just returned from fishing and had edged the canoe to shore.
Grant needed to make a quick trip to the woods, and we
wrestled with his too-tight life jacket, trying to spring him
free. Finally, I got the life jacket off, and he beelined for the
brush to answer nature's call.

That's when I turned around to pull the gear out of the
canoe. It was already fifteen or twenty feet out on the placid
water, drifting away in a light breeze.

My choices were two: plunge into the 50-degree, mid-May water and swim for the canoe, or let it go and consider other options. I had my life jacket on from our fishing. But the day was cold—probably 45 degrees—and I had on nearly all of my warm clothes. They would be soaked. I would be soaked. I would have no clothes as a backup. I would still have a 5-year-old to care for.

Nope. I wasn't going to swim.

Grant returned from the bushes unaware of our evolving situation.

"Grant," I said. "I made a big mistake."

"What, Dad?" he asked.

I pointed at the canoe floating like a wayward feather, now farther out on our bay.

"Oh, no," he said. "What are we going to do?"

That was the question. What were we going to do?

I told him I didn't know for sure yet. That's when he reached for my shoulders, buried his head in my chest, and let the tears flow.

We were about a mile by land from the landing where we had put in and where our car was waiting. The keys to the car, however, were in a pack in the canoe. That would mean an even longer hike to the nearest dwelling.

The chances of another canoe coming by were like the lake we had camped on—slim. We were at the only campsite down a narrow arm off the main body of the lake. We had seen no other people in our day and a half there.

The breeze was light, but it was blowing toward the closed end of the bay. Perhaps the canoe would blow to shore there.

I alternately reassured Grant that everything would be fine and tried to persuade myself that was true.

By now, the canoe had reached the middle of the bay, which was about two hundred yards wide. There it seemed to be caught in the doldrums, spinning first one way, then the other, always slowly. It looked good out there. A red canoe, floating high on the water. It just would have looked a lot better with someone in it.

Then, for just a moment, it appeared to catch some imperceptible breath of wind and drift closer to the far shore of the bay.

"Come on, Grant," I said. "Maybe it'll blow to the other side. If it does, we want to be there when it gets there."

I put his 45-pound frame on my shoulders. He glommed onto my head, pawing my glasses as he ducked the branches we passed. We tried to skirt the shore, but were forced to backtrack and climb a ridge. We dropped to lake level again, tiptoed through some popple blowdowns at the head of the bay, and slogged through some marsh.

Meanwhile, Grant was giving me the play-by-play.

"Yes! Dad, it made it to shore. We can get it!"

We can get it, I thought, if we get there before it blows out again.

On we rumbled, bushwhacking our way along the shore. I could see the canoe just touching a shoreline rock. There was no guarantee the craft would remain there. I barreled on as fast as I dared, trying to guide my passenger through gaps in the branches.

I have been in situations in the bush where I have badly wanted things at times. I have wanted the wind to stop blowing. I have wanted fish to bite. I have wanted bugs to cease and desist. But I don't know that I have wanted anything much more than I wanted to reach that canoe.

Finally, we were there, and the play-by-play boy summed it up for both of us.

"Yes! We made it!"

"But, Dad," he said. "We don't have our life jackets."

You have to admire a kid for thinking that way, but I told him we would be extra careful and go without the life jackets just this once.

We were halfway across the bay when he looked up at me and said, "Well, at least we got our exercise."

We nudged the canoe up on shore. I climbed out and lifted my little buddy with the positive attitude onto shore. He made no move to climb the bank. He stood there on shore, clutching the canoe with both hands.

"It's OK," I told him. "I've got it."

He relaxed his grip, and I pulled the canoe up on shore. I tied it to a tree.

Then we went up and made a quart of lemonade. Before we drank it, we toasted to our good fortune.

Coming and Going

I am leaving home again.

Another trip. Four days this time.

My gear is mostly assembled and sits in duffels or heaps in the house. Lists have been checked and rechecked. My companion will pick me up at five in the morning.

I am full of anticipation, excitement—and sadness.

It did not used to be this way. I used to be focused totally on the adventure that lay ahead of me. But that was in B.C. time: Before Children.

Now, on the eve of a trip, I feel this strange mix of emotions. Part of me wants to be on the trail, to be seeing new country, to expand my horizons in both a physical and a spiritual sense.

But there is the other part of me that feels a distinct twinge of regret about leaving behind those I love.

The night before a trip, I always look in on our sleeping kids. I don't know why. Just to see them one last time, I guess. Because I know I'm going to miss them, and because I know they're going to miss me.

I want to store that last image of them, tucked beneath their blankets, sleeping peacefully, to take with me when I go.

The oldest one, 12, will worry some about me. Before this trip, a winter camping venture, she wants to know if the ice will be good, if I'll be careful, if I'll be OK. I do my best to reassure her, but I know she will worry anyway.

The younger one, 7, will not worry, I think. But he will miss me in the way that he misses his mom when she is gone. At suppertime and bedtime, mostly. And with a vague understanding that something isn't quite complete in his world. At least that's how I imagine it. I have forgotten what it is like to be 7.

I begin to get a sense of what I mean in his life only when I come home. Nearly always, he runs to me and leaps up, throwing his arms around my neck and his legs around my waist, holding me as if he might be able to keep me home forever.

I know, too, when I'm going that it isn't as easy for Phyllis. She's on her own with fixing all the meals, feeding the dog, hauling kids to practices or music lessons or swimming, making sure the trash is put out on Thursdays, packing lunches before school in the morning.

It's a big job. I've done it a few times in her absence, and I know. But we are nowhere even in the trip department. I'm gone much more than she.

Before kids—a long time ago—Phyllis and I would do a lot of these trips together. Or sometimes she would be off on her own when I was gone. Life was simpler then.

Now, in planning a trip, I'll sometimes shorten it by a day or two just to minimize time away from home. Or an overnight trip will be condensed into a long day trip. Sometimes, on winter nights, I'll be hustling down some dark highway just to get home in time to put the kids to bed. One more night means a lot.

A friend of mine, whose husband also gets out frequently, says she can break his life down into five major activities. She enumerates them as she counts on the fingers of one hand—planning a trip, buying food for a trip, packing for a trip, being on the trip and unpacking from the trip. She's kidding. I think.

But I will concede that for some of us, these trips—paddling, fishing, hunting, hiking—are a part of who we are. Making trips into the bush satisfies a need that I hold somewhere deep in my soul. I don't understand it entirely. I know only that being on the trail, living simply, traveling slowly, feeling the rhythms of the land, is something I have to do from time to time.

I'm fine once I'm on the trail.

But the night before, when I'm packed and ready and the little people are sleeping, I have my second thoughts. I watch them sleeping, and they seem almost as vulnerable as they did when they were infants.

I hold those images with me when I'm in the woods, and I'm always left with one thought: Whatever you do, make sure you get home.

Fourteen

The boys are paddling back to camp. Rain has been falling most of the day. Rain gear hangs loosely over their rangy 14-year-old bodies.

But they're happy.

That's David Chapman, up front. His good buddy Brad Bohlman is right behind him. Bringing up the stern is David's dad, Chris. He's somewhat beyond 14. All are from Duluth.

They are smack in the middle of Ontario's Quetico Provincial Park. Dusk is falling on the second day of their week-long canoe trip.

They're returning with good news. They've been out fishing for a couple of hours. Chris Chapman, perhaps as excited as the kids themselves, makes the announcement before the canoe touches rock shoreline.

"We set a personal record," he says.

David takes over.

"I caught a huge bass," he says. "I have it marked on my paddle."

He and Brad scramble out of the canoe. David holds the paddle up horizontally. Brad peers over his shoulder as they search for the scratch David has made on the paddle. They find it. David marks it with a grubby finger as the rest of us—there are seven in all—gather around to admire this phantom smallmouth bass.

The bass would have stretched from the base of the paddle blade to the mark where the blade narrows on the paddle's shaft. Twenty-two inches, give or take a bit.

That's a big bass. Four pounds, anyway. Maybe more.

The fish itself is still swimming. It was released immediately, as is the custom on this trip. Only enough fish for supper—a half-dozen walleyes—are kept.

It has been a good evening on the water. Scott Neustel, another member of the group, estimates the five fishermen who were out caught close to one hundred fish, most of them walleyes.

Someday David and Brad will realize how lucky they are to be part of all this. Now, mostly, it is something of a blur. Ask them what lake they are on, and they might be able to tell you 50 percent of the time. They rarely look at a map. The rest of the time, they are content to be somewhere— anywhere—where the possibility of catching another personal-record walleye or bass or northern pike is imminent.

Already they have been doing this for several years, thanks to David's dad, who makes a Quetico trip every summer. At 14, these boys have caught northern pike over twenty pounds and so many walleyes and bass they have forgotten a lot of three-pounders. The "Lunker Twins," fellow traveler Clint Moen of Duluth has dubbed them.

We have made some tough portages getting to the middle of Quetico this year, but none that measure up to the worst from trips past. At one point, we are slogging through a bog south of McDougal Lake when someone grunts something to David about the difficult going.

"Not as bad as Badwater," he says.

He is talking about a mile-long bog portage in the north-western part of the park that he and Brad have made several times. Old pros at 14.

It is fun having them along, not only for their quiet, strong spirit, but to remind yourself how good it was to be 14 and doing something you love with a good friend. They keep mostly to themselves, especially early in the trip. It probably isn't cool to get too chummy with one of your dad's friends, after all. Some of those old geezers are in their 40s, you know.

But gradually they loosen up and blend with the group. And they know how to work. They'll paddle all day into a wind. They'll haul more than you think a 14-year-old body can haul across a portage. They'll do the dishes if reminded.

The only time they get fussy is with food. They finally balk one night when Moen prepares a thick and tasty split-pea-and-ham soup. David stares at the drab green slurry in the blackened pot.

"Is that stuff really edible?" he asks.

His dad assures him it is. Both boys try to eat it but probably end up going short on calories for the day.

"It's too green," David says.

One afternoon, the boys are coming into camp with David's dad, paddling across a windy expanse of Veron Lake. They have been fishing their way through some small flow-ages throughout the afternoon, catching numerous walleyes and two more bass big enough to notch on David's paddle.

We hear them coming before we see them. From out on the lake comes the sound of singing. Sort of. It is bad singing, but, yes, it is singing. The boys are up front, as always, stroking hard. What they are singing is unintelligible. Possibly that's because David's dad, paddling stern, is doing vocal backup.

The sound must be like nothing else the old pines on Veron Lake have ever heard, but those of us in camp cannot help watching and smiling. What you have is something wonderful happening among a father, a son, and a friend. It has something to do with the fishing, and something to do with the paddling and a lot to do with the joy of being together in good country.

And only one of them understands how lucky they all are.

The other two are busy being 14.

After the Storm

Night has fallen in the canoe country. The four of us have retreated to our tent beneath a cluster of white pines.

Phyllis and I are in the middle, heads propped on stuff, sacks full of clothes. We are reading by the soft glow of our headlamps. The night is cool and damp. Our sleeping bags feel good.

On each side of us, our two children sleep, nestled in their bags. A thunderstorm passed through as the kids got ready for bed, and now it has moved on down the lake.

Lightning still whitens the night occasionally, bleaching for an instant the entire lake and the ridges beyond. Remnant thunder rumbles long and low in the distance. It is a strangely smooth sound, a few miles off. Unlike the ponderous claps that accompanied the storm when it passed over our lake, these are subdued and elongated concussions. They ride over the lakes and hills for long strings of seconds, and lying there in the tent, you can almost visualize them trundling over the land like some gentle giant.

Except for the interludes of far-off thunder, the night is full of silence. The air is thick after the rain, and the night is heavy with quiet.

Once in a while, a light breeze will brush the pines, and a slurry of raindrops will fall against the tent fly. The tent is well pitched, and the fly is tight. The drops sound like someone tapping on the skin of a drum with their fingertips.

This is what we have come for—this silence and peace and absence of intrusion. True, the day before we had heard the muted sound of some engine from the Canadian side of the border a mile north of us. A four-wheeler, perhaps. Or maybe a chain saw. And once, when the wind was right, we could still hear the groan of a truck accelerating up a hill on the Gunflint Trail south of us.

But otherwise, the sounds we heard were more apt to be wind whiffling through pine needles, the chuck of water against rock, or the plop of a bobber landing out on the lake.

Even doing this as regularly as we do, we always find it somewhat remarkable just how much the solitude of the north woods means. We must get awfully accustomed to the sounds of civilization to be struck so forcefully by the contrast we experience in the woods.

This peace, this totally enveloping quiet, is like some sweet nectar you cannot seem to get enough of. Tired as we are, it is impossible not to just lie there in the tent, reading off and on, listening, imagining the night outside.

It is also impossible not to feel exceedingly lucky that we have such an area to visit. It's a place that requires some effort to reach—some paddling, some portaging, some interaction with insects. That is OK. That's what makes you feel different, once you're here, than you would sitting on the deck of someone's cabin.

There are others on this lake, no doubt feeling the same way we are tonight, thinking similar thoughts about the storm, the thunder, the intermittent tapping on the tent. We saw them paddling down the lake earlier in the day. But essentially, we are alone here.

Our children have not been bored, despite the bikes and swimming pools and friends they have left behind. In the middle of the camp, they have created an imaginary restaurant. The 12-year-old often climbs high into a pine. The 6-year-old sits alone for long periods on a rock by the lakeshore. I wonder what he thinks about.

As I put my book away and begin to allow myself to drift away in sleep, I cannot help but think of something our younger child said earlier in the day.

He was just walking through camp, doing nothing in particular, when he said, "I wish we lived here."

The thunder rolls away over the ridges again. Somewhere out on the lake, a loon calls.

Passing It On

Among the possessions my dad left behind when he died last year was a shotgun. It's a Browning 20-gauge, a gun he bought himself for quail hunting about thirty years ago.

When I was home recently, my mom asked my two brothers and me to decide who would take the gun. She isn't planning to shoot any quail, I guess.

I spoke with both of my brothers, and neither expressed an interest in the gun. I brought it home with me.

Understand, this is not a fancy gun, not worth anything as a collector's item. But it's in good condition. I cleaned it up, put some wood polish on the stock, and put the gun away.

Although I would have been happy to draw straws with my brothers to see who might inherit the gun, I will admit that I am quite pleased to own it.

I'm not sure just what it is about these possessions, passed down from a previous generation, that makes them so valuable to us. Some of them—antiques, collectibles—may have value to a broader market as well. But most of what we inherit, I suspect, holds meaning for us only because of its strong association with someone we loved.

For me, this gun is my dad, dressed in canvas pants and a canvas coat, walking up on a plum thicket in his leather boots on a Saturday in October. The gun is also an old, red station wagon, a good pointing dog, and two-track country roads. Looking at the gun, I can hear my dad's gravelly voice, see a covey of quail whirring up from a thicket, and see the steam rising from Dad's thermos of bean-with-bacon soup.

I think, too, the gun helps me remember Dad in a way I want to recall him. He had a tough life in many ways. I realize now that in the years that Dad hunted, hunting made him about as happy as anything he did.

That I am a hunter today only makes the gun more meaningful.

A man I know—not a hunter—said he inherited a somewhat rare model of deer-hunting rifle from his father years ago.

"I take it out of its case about every five years, look at it, and think, 'Dad's gun,'" the man said.

He was smiling.

That is what these hand-me-downs from our parents do for us. They make us smile. When we use a mixing bowl that once belonged to Mom, we feel good about it. When we slip into a wool jacket that Dad once wore, we feel a warmth generated not entirely by the fabric.

I don't know what will happen to Dad's old gun when I am gone. If I hunt for the rest of my life, and my kids come to know me as a hunter, perhaps one of them would like to have it. I would like that.

I suppose Dad would, too.

Snowhouse Snooze

It was a Friday night, and I was beat.

Beat, tired, cold, whipped, done. All I wanted was to go home, eat a warm meal, curl up under a blanket, maybe take a hot bath and read.

I sidled through the kitchen door into the warmth of the kitchen. Home. At last.

Around the corner, on final approach from the dining room, came the flying form of a $4^1/_2$-year-old. He taxied to a stop at my feet.

"Dad," Grant said, "Can we sleep in the snow house tonight?"

Oh yes. The snow house. I had forgotten we had talked about sleeping in the snow house Friday night.

"Well," I said, drawing the word out as long as possible.

I was stalling. Maybe it wouldn't be good for him. Maybe he had been up too late the night before. Maybe his cold wasn't quite done yet.

"We'll have to see," I said.

The parent's cop-out.

Well, after supper, it was time to see. And I couldn't see any good reason we couldn't sleep out.

The temperature was dropping toward zero. The wind was out of the northwest, making the bare popple tops sway.

"Can we?" Grant asked.

"Sure," I said.

We had built the snow house, with the ladies' help, the weekend before. It was a white dome hunkered silently in the far corner of the back yard. Just right for two or three.

At about 8:30 P.M., we began hauling sleeping bags to the snow house. Two for him. Two for me. Two foam pads each. And two candles for light.

So, with Grant in his pajamas and his Barney slippers, we threw our gear on two sleds, kissed the ladies good night, and headed into the dark recesses of the yard.

A snow house is a wonderful place, even without a $4^1/_2$-year-old. It is eerily silent, extremely white and surprisingly warm.

We lit the candles. Cool. A very nice touch.

We snuggled into our bags. Warm. Another nice touch.

I cinched Grant's mummy hood until his face was a smile at the end of a tunnel of goose down and Lite Loft.

He looked out at me from his cocoon.

"Hi, big guy, " he said.

I blew out one candle and began to read by the light of a headlamp.

"Dad," came a voice from the end of the tunnel. "I have to go to the bathroom."

Predictable. Entirely predictable.

Out of the bags, on with his coat. We crawled out the snow house door and stood side by side in the night. Guys, doing what guys do.

We hustled back to the snow house and got Grant snuggled away again.

I spent a few minutes reading, then turned out my headlamp and blew out the last candle. Grant was breathing deeply. Somewhere, far away, I could hear the wind blowing.

Every time I awoke during the night, I would lie in my bags and listen for Grant's breathing next to me. I wasn't worried. Not really. But I needed to be reassured just the same. Maybe he had squiggled too far down into his bags and wasn't getting enough air.

Every time, he was breathing.

In the morning, with daylight coming through our walls of snow, we lay there in our bags for a long time. Waking up. Listening to the wind. Appreciating warmth.

"Ready to go in the house?" I finally asked Grant.

"Not yet," he said.

I never slept in a snow house with my dad. I bet I wouldn't have wanted it to end, either.

The Hunting Life

Plucking a Duck

I sat on a stool, plucking feathers from a teal I shot a day before, three hundred miles away.

The bird was cold in my hand, but soft. The down beneath his breast feathers was thick and dense. It would have insulated the little blue-wing well as he bore south ahead of winter's first serious blasts.

The feathers came off easily in clumps between my thumb and index finger. I shook them into a paper bag at my feet, but not all of them made it. As I continued to pluck, particles of down drifted about in the air and feathers poofed around, if I moved a foot and created a small breeze.

Plucking ducks is not thought of as the most pleasant way to spend time, but I enjoy it if I'm not in a hurry. I like handling all of the game I kill, for reasons that may be both hard to explain and hard to understand.

It seems to me that if you've taken something's life—a serious act—you owe it to that creature to spend some time thinking about it afterward. For me, that time begins almost immediately after I put the bird in my vest. I walk along, the lump of bird warm against the small of my back, replaying all that led up to the moment.

Or maybe it's on some small spit of land or a muskrat house where I'm duck hunting. If the hunting is slow, I'll sometimes pick up a bird I've already shot, just to look at it, stroke its belly, and admire the iridescence of its feathers.

Back home, cleaning birds, the process continues. It may take place under a yard light at some farm on the prairies or on a picnic table in your backyard. The air is cool. You're still wearing the clothes you wore afield or into the slough. The hunt is still wrapped around you.

You cannot help noticing the way an animal is put together when you're handling it. The toughness of a duck's wings, the fuselage-like quality of its breast, the leathery feel of the webbing between its toes. How does a woodcock manage to strut about on the forest floor with such skinny legs? How can a rooster pheasant be so handsome? How many geese—not many, surely—would it take to make a goose-down sleeping bag?

But beyond the mere physical qualities you admire when handling game, you begin to feel this unmistakable connection between the duck marsh or the corn stubble or the popple stand and the meal you will soon eat. Sitting there, plucking a teal, part of you is back at the earthen dike on an October morning with mallards and pintails and widgeon and teal swirling in the sky. There's a dog there, and a friend, and the wind and the cattails and the smell of swamp.

And part of you is stealing ahead to dinner, to that heavy aroma of baked duck, the juices in the pan, the apples and onions stuffed inside the bird, the taste of that dense flesh.

And soon it is all woven together in something that feels like a dream or maybe even religion. It's hard to be sure.

But you've separated this bird from the flock and it is going to help sustain you into another day, and none of us is going to be here forever, and maybe someday, you figure, your own ashes are going to be nourishing the soil that feeds the roots of a big bluestem that shelters the nest of a hen teal that brings off a clutch of chirping ducklings that will one day fly south. And maybe one or two of them will die in order to nourish something or someone else along the way—and all of that seems a lot like a circle.

I finished picking the two teal, and I kept a wing just to look at for a few days. I rubbed the skin of the ducks with salt and stuffed them and put them in the Crock-Pot with a little water. I ate them that night and took my place in the circle with the teal and the pheasants and the grouse and all the others.

Pheasant Camp

The three of us unfold slowly from the red Toyota pickup after six hours on the road. We're stiff, but we're home.

Home, for six days each fall, is an old red farmhouse in Minnesota not far from the South Dakota line. We stand for a moment in the farmyard, letting the silence soak in, looking at all of the sky, smelling the aroma of black dirt and dry cornstalks.

We have come to hunt pheasants and ducks, but mostly what we do is slow down.

A week out here is unlike almost everything we have left behind. Hurry. Responsibility. Deadlines.

Because we bring all of our own food, we never go to town to eat. We do almost all of our hunting within five miles of the farmhouse in Lac Qui Parle County, so we never go to town for gas. If we see another vehicle, it's more likely to be a John Deere than a Ford or Chevy.

The farmhouse sits close to a gravel road and is surrounded by two wetlands, a pasture, picked soybeans, and picked corn. We arrive on a Sunday. It is Wednesday before anyone drives by.

In the course of our week-long visit, we will see far fewer people than we would see during a week in the Boundary Waters Canoe Area Wilderness. Nine, to be exact. We know all of them. Goodman and Marge Larson, who own the farmhouse. The nearby farmers and their families. A fellow hunter from Wisconsin who is a friend of the Larsons.

Six days. Nine people.

We grow accustomed to a silence so profound you can hear a rooster pheasant cackling half a mile away. The darkness at night is so thick that it seems thousands of new stars have been sprinkled in the sky. By day, the countryside is a blend of dusky browns that rolls on forever.

Our peace is enhanced by the schedule we choose to live by here. Our days are defined by the sun. We can hunt ducks half an hour before the sun clears the horizon in the east each morning. We can hunt pheasants until the sun slides past South Dakota on its way west each evening.

When our week is up, we load the dogs and climb back in the truck. When we hit the highway, we're in another world again. Sixty miles per hour seems far too fast. And what is this at the gas station? Someone barking at us over a loudspeaker about pumping gas? The reds and yellows and blues of the convenience store seem grotesquely artificial.

Along the road, somewhere near St. Cloud, a gaudy billboard screams at us. At Tobie's in Hinckley, humanity teems around the clerk's counter. Outside, dueling searchlights violate the night sky, luring gamblers to a casino.

Back in the truck, we ramp up to freeway speed, where we'll live for another year.

Behind the Harvest

I never have felt comfortable with the term "harvest" as it's applied to deer hunting.

Unfortunately, it has become part of the language of the hunt, at least in the voice of the state agencies that manage those hunts. Sometimes, it then becomes the language of the news media that follow the deer hunt.

I try to avoid using it, but sometimes, for the sake of variation within a story, it comes crawling back.

I grew up in country where the harvest was something that happened to wheat or corn or soybeans. It conjures up images of humpbacked green machines eating their way through rolling fields. Something is grown; and when it's ripe, it's harvested. Then a plow comes through, and next spring the cycle begins again.

I just can't picture the deer hunt as a bunch of deer lined up out there in the woods or prairies with blaze-orange reapers grinding through, chewing them up and spitting them out.

Reducing something as personal and quiet as deer hunting to a concept as cold and mechanical as a harvest just doesn't do it for me.

Which, I suppose, is why you don't hear well-layered folks in blaze orange sitting on stools at the Orr Cafe having a conversation like this:

"How's your deer harvest going?"

"Not bad. Have you harvested your buck yet?"

Doesn't happen.

The term "harvest" seems to relate more to numbers than to a bunch of friends gathering in the glow of lantern light. Adding up all the deer registrations is one way to measure a season, but it doesn't say much about what keeps most deer hunters coming back year after year.

Near as I can tell, the best part of deer hunting comes in two forms. Being together. And being alone.

Being together started a long time ago. Maybe a couple generations ago. At least a couple of months ago. It has to do with passed-down .30-30s and old black-and-white photos and a stand where nobody sits anymore.

It has to do with phone calls and food lists and far-flung relatives who always manage to get home in November. Somebody gets there early to roust the squirrels out of the stovepipe and beat the mice out of the mattresses, and pretty soon, the place is warm and crowded and loud.

Then you know it's deer hunting.

Morning comes before daylight, and a bunch of funny-looking bodies start shuffling around in some funky-looking long johns. Sooner or later the wool goes on and the final barbs are issued, along with some quiet but honest words of encouragement. The last person out turns off the lights.

Then it's time for being alone.

With all the warmth of the home or shack inside of them, hunters go forth into the cold and dark. They crunch or slog, depending on the terrain and the morning, until they come to the sitting place. Now the hunt has begun.

You can go out and sit in the woods anytime and listen to the squirrels and the chickadees and those crazy ravens, but there's a big difference between sitting in the woods and hunting.

Now all the little stuff matters. The wind. The silence. The old rifle.

The hunter is alone with all of it. Now it is up to him or her. None of that stuff back at the shack matters now. It's a time for vigilance.

And a time for reflection. While bare branches scratch the sky's belly, a hunter has time to let thoughts ramble back over another year. It's a time for taking stock, for marking another set of seasons, for wondering what the whole ride is about.

Something about all of that quiet and all of that country brings the hunter a little more in tune with what matters most. Thoughts seem clearer, choices broader, courses of action more obvious. Some of that will go home with the hunter when the season is over, the by-product of all that aloneness.

It's good, this season of the deer.

Good to be together again. Good to be alone again.

Too good—far too good—to be simply a harvest.

By the Book

As a single parent, Roxann Lathrop of Remer had a problem. Her 17-year-old son, Brad Holvey, wanted to hunt deer this fall.

Roxann didn't hunt. She knew nothing about deer hunting. Divorced for ten years, she had only last year moved back to Minnesota from California. She had some uncles in the area, but they had grown old and had decided not to hunt.

Roxann, 45, told Brad that maybe someone from their church would be willing to take him hunting.

Brad thought about that.

"No, Mom," he told her. "I want you to go with me. We'll do this just like we've done everything else, just the two of us."

"How could I say 'no?'" Roxann said.

So, together they set about becoming deer hunters.

The subject had come up briefly last fall, only months after they had moved back. But Brad had no gun, and Roxann, just getting by as a substitute teacher, had little extra money. But when sporting goods stores held sales after deer season last fall, mother and son managed to buy some of what Roxann calls "that beautiful blaze-orange clothing."

This summer, Brad's father bought him a 7 mm magnum rifle. Brad saved his money and bought a portable deer stand.

But he and his mom needed to learn something of deer hunting. For that, Roxann and Brad bought books on the subject at a bookstore in Grand Rapids and began reading.

Starting early this fall, they spent part of every weekend in the woods. They knew how to identify deer tracks, buck rubs, and buck scrapes. They sighted Brad's rifle in at a gravel pit.

None of this was exactly what Roxann had planned in the way of quality time with her son.

"Going hunting was not my idea of what I wanted to do at all," she said. "I like the idea of getting meat in those little packages with no eyes looking at you."

But she never hesitated to follow through with her commitment.

"Even if it's not your interest, if it's your child's interest, you should be supportive," Roxann said. "This is like when they get their first tooth or take their first step. You want to be there when they do these things."

Last Saturday morning, when Minnesota's firearms deer season opened at half an hour before sunrise, she was there. They were hunting an uncle's land. Brad was in his portable stand. Roxann was in a permanent stand they had found nearby in the woods. They had with them a book containing directions on how to field-dress a deer.

Brad had no second thoughts about hunting with his mom.

"We've always done a lot together," he said. "I figured our chances were as good as me going out with anybody else."

The woods were crisp, and as soon as Roxann and Brad had settled into their stands, Roxann thought she heard something walking.

"Then I definitely heard something walking," she said. "I saw this deer come up, and my heart started to pound."

She couldn't tell if it was a buck or a doe. Then she lost sight of it momentarily. That must have been when Brad saw it. He could see it was a buck. That's when he got excited.

"I thought he was going to hear my heart beating," Brad would say later.

At 6:50 A.M., eighteen minutes into the season, Brad squeezed one shot from his rifle. Roxann was watching the buck, a four-pointer, when it went down thirty-three feet from Brad's stand, just eighteen feet from hers.

"You did it!" she yelled.

"I was absolutely thrilled," the mother said. "I thought I'd sit and cry like a baby if we got a deer, but I think it was just as exciting for me as it was for Brad."

Once on the ground, they got the book out. Brad unsheathed his knife. Together, on the cold November ground, they figured out how to field-dress a deer.

"It took longer than it must take most people, but we did it," Roxann said.

Just over a year before, they had been living in suburban San Bernadino. Brad, a child of the city, was going to a high school of 2,100. Roxann didn't feel safe going out at night.

That's why she returned to her roots in Minnesota. To Remer, population 396. To what she hoped would be a simpler, better life. This fall, Roxann had landed a full-time job as a special education teacher. She's taking night classes at Bemidji State University to advance her career. She plans to get her master's degree.

Now, she and her son had embraced this deer-hunting challenge and their hands were bloody and they had venison for the winter.

Brad knows deer will not always come so easily.

"I figure it was pure luck to get one in eighteen minutes," he said.

But that isn't the only thing deer hunting has taught him.

"If you put your mind to it," he said, "you can do just about anything, I guess."

Brad's already figuring on hunting next season, too. And he won't have to worry about finding someone to accompany him.

"I'm his partner next year, too," Roxann said. "We're going to do it again."

Close Call

The year had to be 1962. I was a spindly kid of 14, living in Grand Island, Nebraska.

Two things remain etched in my memory from the years I lived in Grand Island. One is that the town is almost perfectly flat, which meant my brother and I could ride our bikes all the way to Riverside Country Club on the outskirts of town.

The other is that I almost shot my dad.

If you are 13 or 14 or 15, and you cannot wait for the day this fall when your parents let you carry a shotgun for the first time, listen up. I know how thrilling it is the first time you get to carry a loaded gun afield for rabbits or partridge or pheasants.

But I also know that I've never felt sicker with a gun in my hands than that November morning outside Grand Island when I was going to get my first shot at a pheasant on the wing.

I was using the gun Dad gave me—the same gun I use today for most of my hunting—a 16-gauge Browning semiautomatic. It was a beautiful gun, made in Belgium. It was light by shotgun standards, but heavy in my adolescent arms. I was probably too small to be carrying a gun like that. A single-shot 20-gauge or .410 would have been safer. But Dad said I could use it, and I was as excited as a 14-year-old has ever been.

Driving into the country, Dad spotted a rooster pheasant in a thicket alongside the gravel road. This was my bird.

"I'll flush it," Dad said. "You stand here on the road and shoot."

I'm sure he set it up that way because he figured it was the safest way to go. I'd have a better shot at the bird from a solid platform—the road—than I would have while trying to negotiate the thick roadside cover. I know Dad figured the chances were darn slim that I'd connect with my target. He probably just wanted me to get the idea of what it was like to shoot at a moving bird under the most controlled circumstances possible.

"Ready?" he whispered.

I nodded.

He rushed into the grass toward the thicket. The bird took flight in a whir of wingbeats. Its flight took it in a line perilously close to my Dad. I raised the gun. I shot.

For a protracted moment, the world stopped. As the smell of gunpowder lingered in the air, both my Dad and I knew something horrible beyond our collective imaginations had nearly happened. The fact that the rooster flew off unscathed over the Nebraska countryside was of no consequence.

Dad turned and looked at me. I don't recall that he said anything. He might have. He wouldn't have had to utter a word.

I'm not sure by how much my charge of lead pellets missed him. I knew only that he had come within a whisker of being a statistic. And I had come within a split second of ruining the rest of my life.

We got back in the car. I'm sure that somewhere on the way home—we hunted no more that day—we talked about what had almost happened. Well, I suppose Dad talked. I mostly did the listening.

I don't recall Dad being furious about what had happened. I don't think he ever raised his voice. It was one of those experiences that carry so much impact on their own that no additional emphasis was necessary.

I was shaky for some time. I was almost physically ill. I could not get out of my head the scenario that might have been—me on the road, my Dad lying in the ditch.

The experience has shaded all the hunting I have done since. I have passed up many shots because I thought a fellow hunter was a bit too close to my line of fire. I have been adamant about making sure I know where my companions are all the time we're in the field. We wear orange caps and vests.

If you are lucky enough to be going afield for the first time this fall—whether you're 15 or 45—and someone takes you aside to talk about being safe, listen to him. This isn't firearms safety class. This is hunting. The real thing.

Live birds do unpredictable things. You can easily lose track of a hunting companion momentarily. Ask yourself this question: Is any shot at a bird worth the possibility of wrecking the rest of your life?

I'm lucky. I learned the answer to that question early, on a gravel road in Nebraska.

Suburban Lust

Each year about this time, I fall victim to a disease.

Suburban envy.

I want a Chevy Suburban. That's right, a one-bedroom apartment on wheels. A gas-guzzling, four-wheeling, trailer-toting, canoe-hauling, duck-decoy-stashing, multi-dog-hauling penthouse for the road.

That's what I need.

The disease presents its symptoms most strongly this time of year, of course, because it's hunting season. The rest of the year, my Plymouth minivan and my aging Camry wagon accommodate my needs just fine.

But if you and a buddy need to load up a couple of dog kennels, four shotguns, two coolers, two sleeping bags, a hundred plastic ducks, food, dog food, waders, and camouflage material, there's really only one vehicle for you. A Suburban.

If there are four of you, the answer is obvious.

Two Suburbans.

Not only would owning a Suburban during hunting season be extremely practical, I think it would change my entire image. You sit up high. You feel good. Suddenly, you're a truck man.

Ever sit in a Suburban? It's like sitting on a couch. Look, over there, across the room. See that guy? He's the driver. We're talking some space here.

Once, I asked a friend of mine with a Suburban if he could help me move a pie cupboard. A major piece of furniture. Wide as a closet, taller than me. I told him we'd probably have to leave it hanging off the Suburban's tailgate, but we could tie a red handkerchief to it.

He showed up. The Suburban ate that pie cupboard. Made it disappear. I'll bet we could have put two of those pie cupboards in there and still have had room for decoys.

Driving a Suburban must be like being captain of an ore boat. You can put that baby on cruise control and slip back to the galley for a cup of coffee and some cinnamon rolls. You can pop open the sunroof, climb up to the deck, and check the weather. You can go aft, check on the dogs, then return to the pilothouse and keep on moving down I-90.

This is a serious vehicle.

There are drawbacks, I know. Twelve miles to the gallon comes to mind. And that's highway driving. But I'm sure any service station could set up a convenient revolving payment plan for gas purchases.

And, yes, you get a Suburban mired down next to a duck slough, and you're going to be making friends with some farmer in a hurry. You'd better hope he's got the biggest John Deere they make, because miring a Suburban is sort of like running an ore boat up on a sandbar.

But I'll risk that.

The real problem with owning a Suburban, as I see it, is the months from December to August. For those nine months, I don't really need a Suburban. I don't need a Suburban for my single-person commute to and from the office. I don't need a Suburban to take two kids to soccer games. I don't need a Suburban to drive the four of us to the Boundary Waters.

A minivan does all of that nicely. And with no second mortgage for gas.

As regularly as I experience Suburban lust this time of year, I've never even bothered going to the dealership to check one out. There's a reason for that.

When I elected, twenty-five years ago, to go into journalism, my professors spoke in lofty platitudes about the craft of writing, the principles of fairness, the importance of accuracy. They neglected to mention that, without holding down two journalism jobs at one time, I wouldn't be able to own a Suburban.

I have come up with a way to solve this problem. A suburban cooperative. Eight, ten, twelve of us will go in together and buy a Suburban. We'll each own shares of it. Like the tires. Or the hood. It'll be like a time-share thing. Maybe someone will need it for a trip to Glacier National Park next summer. Someone else might need it mostly for fishing trips. I'll block out a couple of months in the fall for hunting.

Want in? Give me a call. We'll talk.

Sunrise Grouse

It's six o'clock Sunday morning. The alarm is shrieking at me from somewhere in another world. My arm and hand travel to that world, stifling the sound.

I lie there. The bed is warm. So is my wife. It is only a grouse hunt, I think. I'm not meeting anybody else. I wouldn't have to go.

Once I flip the covers off, I'm able to think more rationally. I will go. The dog needs it.

Dog, heck. I need it.

One does not need to hunt grouse at the break of dawn. Unlike hunting ducks and deer, your odds of surprising a grouse are just as good at mid-morning as they are at daybreak. A lot of hunters consider the grouse a gentlemanly gamebird for that reason.

But over the past couple of years, I have come to believe that sunrise is just the right time to begin a grouse hunt. I'm out of the house by 6:30, slipping shells into the old 16-gauge before 7:00.

I choose a place I hunt too often, but I love it. A winding tote road bisects a stand of adolescent aspen. It hasn't been much for the past couple of years, but then, grouse hunting hasn't been much anywhere for the past couple of years. And when the woodcock are migrating, it isn't uncommon to find that thirty or forty of them have pitched into this one-time clear-cut to waddle the forest floor and mine the soil for worms.

I put a small cowbell on the dog to keep track of her in the dense woods, and I wince at the way the clanking shatters the silence of the morning.

The morning is just as I have hoped it would be. Frost again during the night. A half-moon still suspended high in the west. Air thin and sharp.

We move into the aspen. I follow the yellow canine blur and her trail of sound.

When the sun comes up, the illuminated sides of the aspen trunks turn the color of honey. The backsides remain shadowed and gray-green. Against the sunlight, every leaf is etched and gilded.

The earth smells like dead wood and damp leaves and things that have been dying here for ten thousand years. It pulses through my nostrils on cool jets of desiccated air, and I cannot get enough of it.

This is why I come at dawn. It is not that I think I will see more birds by hunting at this hour, although I seem to see plenty. It is that I love the way the woods feel when the day is in its infancy. If you can see enough birds and shoot them against a backdrop that lets you remember each one more clearly, then I'd rather do it that way.

The first bird takes flight when the dog's nose gets too close. I wave at the grouse with the shotgun, and see the fleeing form fall from the sky. The dog comes snuffling back with it. The warmth of the bird in my hand seems to further define the cool of the morning, and, as always, I look at the creature for a long time. I don't know what I expect to see. The bird is unremarkable compared to other grouse. But I am not ready for the experience to be over, not ready for that final act of slipping the bird into my vest.

I pluck a couple of loose feathers from the grouse, let the Lab smell the bird again, and then slide it into the game pouch.

The second bird is unshootable. The third flushes in front of the dog and flies straight at me for a second or two. It is a view of a grouse one seldom sees—the crested head, the cupped wings, the flaring tailfeathers.

It unnerves me, and when the bird finally presents a going-away view, I miss badly. But I may keep the memory of that head-on encounter longer than I'd have remembered the meal.

I try to explain to the dog why there is no bird to bring back, but she doesn't seem to care. It is not as if she hasn't witnessed the situation before.

We move on, seeking more birds. At one point, the dog seems to get scent and I am knifing through the woods with abandon trying to keep up with her. The bird never materializes, but there is a moment in that minichase when we're moving directly at the sun.

The scene is golden. All I remember is dew falling from the golden leaves, steam rising from the dog's creamy back, the cloud of her breath hanging behind her, sunlight washing over all of it.

This single image, this fleeting moment, presents itself and is gone in less than a second. Yet I may never forget it.

That is why I hunt grouse at dawn.

Full Circle

During November 1997, Aaron Kerola of Cloquet wounded a big buck near Cook and had almost tracked it down when another hunter killed it.

This happened during the opening weekend of Minnesota's firearms deer season. The eight-pointer was not only the first deer Aaron had ever shot at in three seasons of deer hunting. It was the first deer he had ever seen while hunting.

Aaron and his friend Chris Stevens expected the worst when they encountered the man who dropped the buck. They thought he would claim it as his own. But the man, who Aaron described as being "about 60," let the boys have the buck, gave them a rope to drag it out of the woods, and hauled the buck and the boys back to their camp in his pickup.

Aaron never got the man's name. A week went by.

On the second Monday of the season, after the story appeared in the *Duluth News Tribune*, a hunter from Nashwauk called. He said one of his hunting partners, Carl Schultz, was the man who had shot the buck and helped the young hunters.

Schultz, who lives in Angora, said that the boys weren't far behind the buck when he shot it. He came down from his stand and approached Aaron and Chris.

"I said to one of them, 'That new Buck knife of yours looks pretty sharp. Now you'd better gut your deer with it,'" Schultz said.

He said Aaron looked at him and said, "My deer? You're going to give me that deer?"

Schultz didn't bother to tell the boys about something he'd been carrying with him for nearly three decades.

"When I was about the same age as those boys, I shot the biggest buck I ever shot in my life. But I lost it," said Schultz.

Schultz had wounded the deer, a big farmland animal he estimated to weigh more than two hundred pounds. He was tracking it, just as Aaron and Chris were tracking theirs, when he heard a shot. Another man had killed the buck. Schultz pleaded his case, but the man would have none of it.

"The guy wasn't going to give me the deer," Schultz said. "He said flat out, 'I killed it. That's my deer.' I always figured if I ever saw something like that, I wasn't going to take the deer."

He doesn't regret it for a moment.

'I got a bigger charge out of watching those two boys be so excited," he said. "They must have thanked me a thousand times."

That morning wasn't the only time Schultz had seen the big buck. He had seen it several times while bow hunting near Cook, he said, but he couldn't get a shot at it.

His party of seven hunters ended up getting five bucks that fall. None of them measured up to Aaron's buck.

Schultz had read the story in the newspaper paper but declined to call and turn himself in as the good guy in this scenario. He isn't that kind of guy, say those who know him.

Schultz did, however, get a chuckle out of Aaron's guessing Schultz's age at "about 60."

Schultz is a mere 53.

Then again, doing the kind of thing Schultz did for Aaron might easily make a guy feel seven years younger.

Deer Camp Characters

Take your average North Country deer camp. Minnesota. Wisconsin. Doesn't matter.

What you've got here, near as I can tell, is a collection of characters. If you've been there, you know the ones I'm talking about.

One's your Uncle Milt. One's your brother Gene. One's his kid, Pete. And, yes, one is you.

Over the years, as they come up through the ranks and take their places in the camp, each cultivates his own hunting personality and must bear the weight of his own reputation.

Here they are, then. See if these folks seem like hunters you recognize. I've chosen to put all of them in the male gender, though I recognize that a lot of women hunt deer, too. Feel free to inject a liberal supply of feminine pronouns where they apply in your own camp.

First, let's look at Mr. Gadget.

That's him coming there on the new four-wheeler. The one with the GPS unit on its handlebars. Mr. Gadget may not always get his deer, but he always gets the latest gizmo designed to improve his hunting.

Life has been good for Mr. Gadget lately. The catalogs, magazines, and store shelves are full of stuff this guy needs. And he needs this year's model. The four-wheeler and the GPS are just a start. He's also likely to be the one with the winch, the combination wristwatch/compass, the remote timer to track deer movements, the latest scent dispensers, the grunt call, and the antlers to rattle.

You give him a bad time, but when it's time to haul out your buck, who you gonna call to borrow the four-wheeler? That's right. Mr. Gadget.

Which brings us to . . .

Mr. Catalog Model. He's a close relative of Mr. Gadget, but he prefers to put his money into soft goods—deer-hunting apparel. He's never worn out a piece of deer-hunting gear because he's always bought a new one—on sale after the season—before the old stuff could wear out. Blaze-orange bibs to big-foot boots, Mr. Catalog Model has it all.

Electric socks. Synthetic longies. Earflap caps. Combo mitten-gloves with special "shooting fingers." Sweaters. Vests. Parkas.

And Mr. Catalog Model knows what they're made of. Thinsulate. Fleece. Polartec. Primaloft. Microfleece. Down. Gore-Tex. Supplex. Tenmile Cloth.

Wool? What's that? Doesn't that come from an animal? Mr. Catalog Model has no need for that.

Look sharp, feel sharp, hunt sharp. That's Mr. Catalog model.

Have we mentioned Mr. Ballistics?

He doesn't care what he looks like. Isn't into gimmicks. But if you want to know the muzzle velocity of a 170-grain .30-30 Winchester, ask Mr. Ballistics. He can speak feet-per-second. Knows your recommended payloads for your .270s, your .30-30s, your .300s, your 7 mm magnums, your .30-'06s.

Knows them? He's loaded them. Customized the powder loads. Experimented with primers. Patterned them at 50, 100, and 150 yards.

Mr. Ballistics has stacks of reloading magazines at home. He never throws them out. Might need one from, say, 1984.

When Mr. Ballistics kills a deer, he doesn't just want to know it's dead. He wants to know what the bullet did once it hit the animal. This is not blood-lust. This is ballistics.

Of course, we don't want to forget Where's My Flashlight? This is the guy who brings all the required stuff to deer camp, then can never find it. Why? Because it's all over. On Dean's bunk. By the woodstove. Outside. In a vest pocket. Left on his deer stand. Left behind in his vehicle. Left behind on his porch at home.

He means well. He's a decent guy. But Where's My Flashlight? drives the rest of us crazy. Whenever he's missing something, he assumes we know where it is.

"Have you seen my shells?"

"What happened to my cap?"

"Did I leave my gloves over here somewhere?"

Sooner or later, it's inevitable: We start hiding things from Where's My Flashlight? We can't help it. We know it drives him crazy. And for some reason, that makes us happy.

While most of these camp characters seem to exhibit negative or questionable qualities, to be fair we must look at the other side, too. Which is where we meet Mr. Gets His Deer.

Doesn't matter what the weather is. Doesn't matter how many wolves are around. Doesn't matter what the "deer numbers" are.

Mr. Gets His Deer always gets his deer. He isn't flashy. He doesn't brag about it.

His clothes are old. He owns no gadgets. But he can sit on a stand all day. Sooner or later, Mr. Gets His Deer is going to see a deer. And when he does, he's going to shoot it. It's that simple.

We rarely give Mr. Gets His Deer any grief. There are two reasons for that. One is that he never gives anybody else any grief, and it's no fun to bug someone who doesn't bug you back.

And second, we can't afford to hassle Mr. Gets His Deer. In the lean years, it's his venison we're eating.

Which brings us, finally, to Mr. Camp Chef. No camp would be complete without one. Who's the guy who's up at camp the week before, making sure there's wood for the stove? Mr. Camp Chef. Who goes up on Thursday before opener to open things up and stock the cupboards? Mr. Camp Chef. Who has the shack smelling like Grandma's kitchen on Thanksgiving every night when you come dragging in cold and tired from the stand? Mr. Camp Chef.

Oh, he'll hunt some. After he's cleaned up from the pancake-and-sausage breakfast.

He'll hunt again for a while after lunch, as long as he remembered to thaw out the roast. But 'long about 3 o'clock, he's heading for the shack to get started on the appetizers and the entree.

We love deer hunting. We love the shack. And we love Mr. Camp Chef.

One word of warning about Mr. Camp Chef. He doesn't mind cooking for you. He's happy to sacrifice a little hunting to put out the spreads he does. Just don't try to help him. That's the only way you get crosswise with Mr. Camp Chef. Sit back. Sip a cool beverage. Ask him if you can bring in more wood for the stove.

But don't get in his way.

Did we miss anyone? I didn't think so.

Happy hunting. Here's hoping all the regular characters show up at your camp again this fall.

The Hidden Hunt

All they see are the deer, southbound, legs hanging stiffly from the backs of the trailers. Or our orange forms behind the wheels of pickups. Or clusters of us back at the truck, exchanging reports from the morning hunt.

They see us trudging about in our heavy boots, wearing our layers of orange, lugging our rifles. When they see us, we often look cold or tired. Because we are.

You would like to tell them they are not seeing the real deer hunt. You would like to tell them about the kind of quiet that can make a gray jay's wingbeats seem loud, the call of a raven absolutely raucous. You would like to tell them about a chickadee that looked you in the eyes or a grouse you watched for half an hour.

You would like to sit them down and tell them about the perverse kind of joy that comes from freezing for four hours in the afternoon and then warming yourself around a woodstove for four hours in the evening.

Cold? You bet you get cold. No matter what the boot makers claim or what kind of synthetic miracle fiber they put in parkas these days, November cold still finds a way in if you give it long enough. And you always give it long enough, because that is the one thing you have on your side: time.

Time and love. If you wait long enough, if you have elected to sit in the right place, if you have read the sign correctly, sooner or later a lovesick buck will come bumbling by. The doe will have already been by, and she will be all he has on his mind. Head down, neck extended, he will for these few minutes have put caution on hold.

Then, if you have remembered to brush the snow from your scope and managed to remain vigilant and held off the temptation to climb down and get your blood circulating again, you will have your moment.

Still, it comes with no guarantees. So much can happen. The slightest creak. A too-quick movement. The shuffle of a cold boot. The buck did not grow eight points being dumb. If you make one more mistake than he does—well, you know the rest.

You would like to tell them that, too. That this is not a sure thing. That sometimes it is days between sightings. That even with a dependable rifle and a good scope and today's ammunition, it is not a sure thing. Not a given. Which is part of why you do it.

There is precious little left these days with the wonder left in it. Not much remains that is wild and unpredictable and natural. So every year you sit out there in that tree, reaffirming what you had forgotten since last November.

What you remember again is that after three or four days out there, you begin to feel about as good as you ever feel. Life has been reduced to these essentials—eating, sleeping, hunting. You finally begin to slow down. You have rekindled the old skills of watching and listening. You have become as much a part of the forest as a human is ever allowed to become.

Some would say the hunting is secondary, that it is the companionship of the camp and the solitude of the forest that matter most. But you know better. It is the hunt that makes all the rest of it happen, that deepens the ties to your fellow humans, that unites your gang for those few days each November. Yeah. The hunt still matters very much.

Getting a deer? That's nice. It takes the experience to another level. Completes some time-honored connection to the land. Seals some pact you made long ago with the four-leggeds.

It also makes a lot of winter meals much more satisfying in a way that goes beyond the taste of venison.

That is some of what you would like to tell them when they drive by, staring at you in your blaze orange by the side of the road.

Dog Tales

Puppy Love
First Retrieve
HMOs and Lab Riders
Just for Fun
Yellow-Dog Years

Puppy Love

For years, Phyllis has been saying, "Sam, you need a hunting dog."

And I'd say, "Oh, honey, I can get along without a hunting dog. I don't really want one. My friends have good hunting dogs. A dog is such a chore to take care of and all."

"No," she would say. "You need a hunting dog. And don't get a small one. Get a big one. One that will lie on the floor here in the kitchen and slobber a lot and track in mud."

Well, maybe that isn't exactly the way the conversations went. The details escape me.

All I know is that now our enclosed back porch has several wet spots and several muddy pawprints on the floor. Banjo has come to live with us.

She's a yellow Labrador that, at nine weeks, has legs the size of sapling maples and feet that could stomp out forest fires. We can only hope she doesn't grow into them.

Actually, hunting was only a secondary reason we got Banjo. The first was that we thought we needed more activity in our life. We just didn't think that one full-time job, one part-time job, a cat, and kids 8 and 3 were quite enough. We had all this spare time on our hands, and we thought, "How could we best use this time?"

Well, it was so obvious. We needed a small mammal.

I mean, what could be more logical than housebreaking a dog and potty-training a child at the same time?

The first few days, the women in the family were gone. It was just the 3-year-old and Banjo and me. And Freckles the cat. Basically, it was a zoo with a couple of humans thrown in for laughs.

Banjo spent most of those first days walking around about six inches behind the 3-year-old's rear end, trying to get a bite of it. Which she did on numerous occasions. But the real problem was the mittens. These are the strung-through-the-jacket-sleeves kind of mittens that 3-year-olds often wear.

The mittens tend to hang about nose-high on Banjo, which is convenient. And they're loose wool, so her teeth— roughly the sharpness of that scraping hook your dental hygienist uses—catch nicely.

One day, getting ready to leave, I left the 3-year-old and Banjo on the driveway together while I went back into the house for something. Next thing I hear is a high-pitched wail. That would be the 3-year-old, I thought. I looked out. There was the 3-year-old, prone on the driveway, one arm extended. Out of the sleeve of the jacket on the extended arm ran a taut blue string, and at the end of the string was a taut mitten, and at the end of the mitten was a yellow furball—head low, tail high—tugging like crazy.

It hasn't been all heartwarming moments like that one, though. There have been some trying times, times when I want to say, "Phyllis, are you sure this is what you want?"

Friends have been encouraging.

"This puppy stage only lasts a couple of years," one said.

"You know what they say," another lady said. "When you get a Lab, get a two-by-four to train it."

And my personal favorite: "You know, Labs have drool glands instead of brains."

Oh, and did I mention the cat? Freckles has spent most of our Two-Weeks-Since-Banjo-Came striking her Halloween-Cat pose. The arched back. The bared fangs. The thick tail.

All Banjo wants to do is be her friend, but Freckles will have none of it. When Banjo flops over too close, Freckles raises a clawed paw in defiance. Banjo then raises his paw, trying to play the game. It looks like they're trying to give each other high fives.

My greatest fear is that Banjo will imprint on the cat. We'll be out there in pheasant country, hot on the scent of a running rooster pheasant, and when she gets close to the bird, she'll suddenly freeze, arch her back and raise a paw.

Oh, well.

At least Phyllis is happy now.

First Retrieve

So, we went out, the pup and I, to see if we could find the sole remaining ruffed grouse in northern Minnesota.

I share this in the spirit of all those who have gone afield for the first time with a coming-of-age pup, whether yellow or black or spotted, whether retriever, setter, or spaniel. Nothing quite measures up to that first time you open the tailgate and introduce forty or fifty pounds of energy to a new world of smells.

This is the hunt. The real thing.

To be sure, there is plenty that has come before—the early socializing, the obedience training, the help and advice of many friends. Now it is time to make the next logical step.

I try to remember: to my pup, the sight of a butterfly is likely to be as compelling as the scent of a gamebird. That is what we were out to change, with the help of a few ruffed grouse.

This is not the ideal year to be getting a young dog acquainted with the game of hunting. I've talked to too many hunters who have put lots of miles on their boots without flushing even a single grouse. To imagine that we would go out, put up a few birds, and have the pup come to understand the sequence—scent, flush, shot and retrieve—was more than optimistic.

But you can toss training dummies in the backyard for only so long before you have to see if the scent of a wild bird triggers the synapses in that doggie brain.

We drove north for an hour or so into the Isabella country. It's big and quiet and, most years, home to a fair number of grouse. We found one of those lovely back roads on which you have to dodge emerging boulders and skirt popple snags that the last windstorm pruned from the forest. We drove the road until we found a four- or five-year-old clear-cut growing back to doghair aspen, and we got out and walked.

For starters, the pup had to learn that she was to be out in front and that I would bring up the rear. She kept looking over her shoulder as if to say, "Hey, are you ever going to catch up?"

And I kept telling her that, no, this was how it worked— the dog goes first. All I wanted was for her to come across whatever it is that grouse leave behind when they stroll on a carpet of popple leaves, some tiny little molecules of grouse scent that for the past century or so have been sending charges of excitement through the fiber of Labrador retrievers.

But, no.

We spent most of three hours not crossing any grouse-scent molecules. Not even an atom or an electron. We worked high ground and low. We worked younger aspen and older patches.

We were back in the car, having just taken another long walk with the shotgun, when I looked up the road and saw a

grouse standing in the middle of it. Sometimes, you figure
the bird-dog gods are smiling down on you, saying, "OK,
partner. There you go. We're offering up this grouse for you
and your pup. Use it wisely."

"Banjo," I said to the snuffling sound in the portable kennel, "we're going to shoot a grouse."

The question was how to let the dog out of the kennel so
she could see the bird flush, watch the shot, and see the bird
fall. No, that wasn't the real question. The real question was
how, if I let Banjo out of the kennel, I was going to get within
shooting range of the bird before the dog homed in on it like
a Patriot missile wearing yellow fur.

We were going to see if all that practice with the "sit" and
"stay" commands was worth anything.

I let the dog out and told her to sit in the road. She could
see the bird about thirty yards away. I told her to stay, and
walked away as if I knew she would.

She did.

The bird turned out to be a spruce grouse, a species not
known for its elusive traits. It flushed on schedule. I shot it. It
fell in the woods.

I called the dog, who beelined to where a light shower of
grouse feathers was drifting to the forest floor. She snuffed
around in those feathers like a teenage girl sampling cologne at
the mall. She snorted them. She licked them. She nuzzled them.

The bird had fallen about five yards beyond the feathers,
and I waited in the road for the pup to figure that out. She
was hunting hard and made a big circle through the woods
and back to the road. She found the ejected shotgun shell I
had fired and brought it to me, carrying it as if she were smok-
ing a cigar. I took it and thanked her.

Then, coming to my senses, I called her downwind of the
dead grouse and let her nose do the rest. By the time she

found the bird, beneath three young balsam firs, I was standing out in the road again. She picked up the grouse, trotted out in the road, and dropped the bird at the feet of the happiest human in the Northern Hemisphere.

I have talked to many hunters since that day. All of them can remember precisely the place and the details of their dog's first retrieve. I'm not surprised.

I won't see many more grouse this fall. I may not shoot another one. I don't care.

On a quiet back road, on a sunny afternoon in October, my pup became a retriever.

HMOs and Lab Riders

There's been a lot of talk coming out of Washington about health care lately. Single-payer plans. HMOs. Universal care.

But near as I can tell, our nation's leaders are skirting the real issue. We're talking about dog health insurance.

This was brought to my attention when I heard about a man whose yellow Labrador retriever had eaten a rope and a diaper. Or tried to. The payload never did clear the animal.

Vet bill: $1,800.

Clearly, we have a need for some kind of policy to cover our critters. Eighteen hundred bucks is a lot of money. You might be saying, "Well, it's just a dog." Sure, it's just a dog— if it's someone else's dog. If it's a dog you've whelped and loved and trained and suffered beside in duck blinds for several years, it's a clear-cut decision: You'll forgo your vacation, but the dog will get fixed.

So, I propose a new definition for HMO: Hound Maintenance Organization. A bunch of vets gets together, sets up a group plan, and hound owners sign up. We pay a small monthly fee, and when old Buck gets to hurting, we've got that convenient 80/20 co-pay to bail us out.

This HMO would cover all of your routine dog ailments. Getting hit by cars. Porcupine quill removal. Hip replacements. Barbed-wire-fence lacerations. And gastrointestinal complications resulting from eating (a) wood products, (b) road-killed squirrel, (c) leftover chicken parts still in the plastic wrap and (d) toy items given away with Happy Meals.

OK, you're saying, not all dogs are as dumb as Labs. I own a Lab. I hear you. So we'll have one plan for your basic dogs—your pointers, your European breeds, your high-rent dogs. Then we'll have the Lab rider. It's a few extra bucks, but it's worth it. Call it Major Medical.

In my case, I'd push for a dental plan, too. My dog eats the chain-link in her dog kennel.

"She's got some scouring here on her teeth," my vet said during one examination of the dog. "Does she chew on metal?"

Well, yeah. Sign me up for the dental plan. You don't want a canine without canine teeth.

Now. There's one other area that needs to be covered, and I'm not sure what category this falls under. But it's very important. Sort of like the liability portion of your auto coverage.

This is needed to cover Things The Dog Destroys on the way to requiring medical attention. Such as motel curtains. Truck steering wheels. Couch cushions in homes of people you're staying with. Carpet. Chickens. Pies left out on the porch to cool. Leather gloves. Shoes.

Mostly, dogs destroy these things by chewing on them, but there are other creative ways they've found to cause damage, too. Such as leaping through the glass window of a pickup topper.

If you think I'm making up any of these problems, talk to any dog owner.

When you're through laughing, write your congressperson. We're going to need all the help we can get on this one.

Just for Fun

When I saw the notice in the newspaper, I thought, "What's the worst that could happen?"

You put on your cross-country skis, you hook yourself up to an overrested yellow Lab, and you try to cover two and a half miles as fast as you can. What could go wrong?

The notice that caught my eye was an announcement of a series of ski-joring "fun races" in Duluth. Ski-joring is a Norwegian word that, loosely translated, means "broken skis likely, poles too, yah, sure."

The Sunday afternoon races are sponsored by the Duluth Pack Store, which happens to sell real ski-joring equipment, and Snowflake Nordic Center, which agreed to regroom its trails after a dozen or so canines left night deposits, if you know what I mean.

Being an experienced Lab owner, I considered some of the possible scenarios that might occur. Let's list them:

1. Dog eats harness.
2. Dog eats another dog.
3. Dog eats another skier.
4. Skier loses finger breaking up dog fight.
5. Dog and skier start race together, but only one finishes race—the dog.

So, I plunked down my five bucks and signed up.

Before the race, a dozen of us stood around with our four-legged partners. There were several huskies, a couple of Labs, an Airedale, a springer spaniel, a collie, and a German short-haired pointer.

I noticed that several of my fellow competitors seemed to be serious about ski-joring. They had purchased actual ski-joring waist harnesses with quick-release hitches. Why, I wondered, would a quick-release hitch be important?

No fancy harness for me. My waist belt was a piece of webbing we once used to hold our infant children in their high chairs. I had a dog harness for Banjo, and I pieced together some webbing that would connect the two of us.

We had done this once before, on a lake, and it had gone well except that Banjo, our Lab, kept pulling to the side rather than straight ahead. That was no problem on a lake. I was concerned about the implications of that problem on a ski trail and found myself thinking again about that quick-release hitch.

The race got off to a good start. We left the starting line at one-minute intervals, which allowed the suspense to build for a while before we encountered each other on the trail. That's where the race proved interesting.

"I'll pass you on the left," I hollered to a man with a black Lab whom we came upon.

I moved to the left. Banjo, however, decided to pass on the right. I remember just missing the man as I changed direction. A small tangle ensued, and Banjo took advantage of the down time, piling into the deep snow along the trail to cool off.

I pulled her back onto the track, and off we went again. Around the next corner, two other racers were trying to disentangle themselves and their dogs from one another. One skier was just completing a couple of 360-degree revolutions on his skis to get his dog's lead line unwound from his waist.

What he needed, I thought, was a quick-release hitch.

On we went. A woman with a dog named Pecos came up on Banjo and me. I moved over to let them pass. Pecos, however, was content just to be near us. The joy, Pecos seemed to think, was merely in catching up to other racers.

"She just wants to chase," her owner said.

Twice the woman and Pecos tried to pass us. Twice Pecos eased to a trot. The last time I saw the woman during the race, Pecos was gaining on us again, but the woman's waist belt seemed to come apart without warning. Probably a problem with a quick-release hitch.

Banjo had, by that time, decided racing was an exercise in excess. I skied ahead of her for at least half the race, coaxing her to run alongside, at the least, if she wasn't going to pull.

We finished that way, both of us panting hard. Afterward, I was looking around for the windbreaker I had left near the starting line, when a woman pointed it out to me.

"It's over there," she said. "I hate to say this, but a collie peed on it."

Yellow-Dog Years

My dog is dog-tired. This is the fourth day of a six-day pheasant hunt, and she is wearing down.

Late afternoon now. We hunted hard in the morning, flushing only hens, which are off-limits to hunters. I knew if I let her hunt right after our lunch, she would expend herself completely, so we both rested—something rare on this week in western Minnesota.

My two partners, whose dogs flushed roosters this morning, have shot their two-bird limits today. Now it is our turn. We leave the little farmhouse about 4:30 P.M., with a couple of hours of daylight to hunt.

Banjo knows what we are up to. At $2^1/_2$, the yellow Lab has finally come into her own as hunter. We work through some chest-high switch grass, finding some weak scent attached to no live birds.

We skirt some cattails and cross a low meadow, heading for a grassy hillside on the east side of this half-section we hunt. But as we near the end of some standing corn rows, Banjo's pace picks up. She is pulled along, nose to the ground, into the corn. This is the lone pheasant hunter's worst nightmare. Chances are the birds will lure the dog deep into the corn, where the hunter cannot keep track of her. But this time, as fate would have it, it is different. Banjo enters the corn only a few feet from the row ends and comes charging my way, vacuuming hot pheasant scent.

I know what all of her signals mean—the knitting of her brow, the perk of her ears, the hyper wag of her tail, the intensity in her eyes. The rooster is up within seconds, out of knee-high grasses, clattering behind me and over the corn. The bird is young, just getting his rooster colors, but he is a rooster. The old 16-gauge does what it has done plenty of times. A two-shot bird. Banjo is on the pheasant at once, lifts it gingerly, returns it on a trot.

There were times, many times, I wondered if we would ever get to this point, Banjo and I. This partnership started on the forty-ninth day of her life. We did everything the book said to do, mostly on schedule. We learned from friends and Duluth retriever guru, Joe DeLoia. But for a period of that first year, I had a Lab that didn't like to get in the water. For a long time, I had a Lab that showed little interest in retrieving dummies. Twice I waded pocket-deep into ponds to retrieve dummies she chose not to bring to me.

For a period, she was happy to pick up a bird that had been shot, but she had no great interest in delivering it to me in a direct fashion. I remember the words of Pat LaBoone of Clear Creek Outdoors on one such occasion, as he witnessed Banjo performing a plodding, circuitous retrieve of a rooster pheasant.

"It's like a guy told me one time," LaBoone said. "There are no dogs that won't retrieve. There are some dogs that won't come."

We went home and worked on "come." Now she comes.

Understand, this is nothing that hundreds of other hunters and dog owners haven't done. For years, I listened to them tell me that without a dog, they probably wouldn't hunt anymore. Now I know. Watching the dog, admiring the dog, loving the dog, being amazed by the dog—that is what the hunt has become for me.

I slip the young rooster into my vest. Banjo is already off, up the swale. When we left the house, she was hardly interested in walking. Now she is a honey-colored blur in the switch grass, quartering on a gallop.

I move along, reading her as she translates the scents for me. Nothing here now. Wait a minute. Could be. No. Field mouse, maybe. Over here. A hint of pheasant. Nothing solid. No trail. Here now. Yes. The real thing.

She snuffles deeply in one spot, determines the bird's direction of travel, and we're off. A steady trot. Intermittent bursts of speed. My hopes rise. She weaves back and forth—sniffing, sorting, sifting.

Finally, we reach crescendo speed. When she begins to get more vertical in her posture, almost gathering herself as if to pounce, bounding from side to side in short hops, I know the flush is imminent.

There. Up. A riot of wing beats. I plant my feet, raise my gun.

Hen.

"No bird, girl," I wheeze, and I whistle her back in.

This, I figure, will do her in. She has to be spent now. Done in. Exhausted.

We move on through the grass. She is panting hard now. I need to get her water, but we are a quarter-mile from the nearest pond or willow thicket.

I kneel in the grass for a moment and make Banjo rest with me. I am humbled by her desire. I have heard of dogs that hunted until they dropped and were carried from the field—alive but overextended. It would scare me to violate that trust with my dog, to have asked too much of her so that I might keep hunting. But how does one know where that line is? How does one know that one more chase is one too many?

Banjo and I rise, get moving again. We will work as directly as possible to a pond, but we might as well work through the rest of this light grass. It is knee-high to waist-high switch grass, yellow-gold, and I must keep a close eye on the dog not to lose track of her. We are nearing the end of the grass when she hits the scent. Some scent trails are weak and must build as the chase continues. This is hot from the moment she crosses it.

We are off on a wild romp. A zig. A zag. A sprint. A tight circle. Another sprint. For most of a minute, which seems like half an hour, we do this.

The rooster comes off Banjo's nose, and time slows to a crawl. I try to get my feet beneath me. The bird is escaping left to right, my least likely successful shot. But we need this bird. Need it to finish the day, let my dog rest, let her drink and then sleep on the rug back at the red farmhouse.

It seems minutes before I get the gun up. The first shot is behind the bird, but on the second report, the bird tumbles from the sky. Banjo has followed all of this, the gaudy trajectory of flight, the shot, the fall. She is there. I have complete confidence she will find the bird. I stand, waiting. When I see her coming, I call her gently just to make sure she knows where I am.

I am so happy. Not just to have made the shot, although that is important. But happy about all of it. The magic of a dog's nose. The instinct that allowed her to track the rooster. The wild abandon of the chase. The complete unpredictability of what would happen, and when. The way we have come to be together in this hunting partnership, Banjo and I.

I am filled with an elation I have felt on other rare moments in my life—the birth of a child, falling in love, skiing or running to exhaustion, paddling a challenging white-water drop.

Banjo stands before me with the bird, and I take it from her mouth. She sputters a couple of feathers and stands there, panting hard. I kneel beside her, try to hug her, want to let her know how much she means to me. She has no time for such sentiments. She merely wants to continue hunting.

The bird is beautiful in a way that seems to have been reserved for pheasants, brook trout, arctic char, and wood ducks. I hold it, smooth its russet feathers, thank it for being part of this timeless equation.

Then I stow it and head for the pond.

Voices from the Land

Without Jim
Margaret's River
The Frugal Fly Fisher
Shared Passions
Travels with Charlie

Without Jim

We can still see Jim Keuten there, rocked back in the old gray swivel chair in the back room at Jim's Bait. Several of the regulars would be gathered around, holding cups of coffee on their knees. Elsie would be sitting across from Jim at the little countertop, working on one of her projects, her hands always busy.

Occasionally, the bell on the front door would jingle, and someone would come through. Jim would get out of his chair and sidle toward the front room to see if someone needed help. Likely as not, the new arrival would be someone headed for an empty chair in the back room, where heads would nod in greeting and the conversation would continue.

Many of us in the Duluth fishing community are still trying to grasp the fact that Jim will never be a part of that scene again.

Jim, who with his wife Elsie was the longtime proprietor of Jim's Bait in Duluth, died Monday. A memorial service was held yesterday.

In the days since Jim's death, many of us have tried to console each other over the loss of a man who represented so much that is so good about life. As so many of the people have said in the past few days, Jim was perhaps the most honest, fair, and generous person you could ever hope to come across.

Granted, there are plenty of good people around, but Jim's benevolence touched a part of our lives—fishing—that is all wrapped up in wonderful places, treasured stories, and the best of times.

Your accountant might be good and honest and fair, but you just don't sit around swapping stories about debits and credits.

Honesty is worth a lot in the bait business. The fishing world in general is tainted with the aura of—well, let's just call it exaggeration. It is in the best interest of bait and tackle shops that the fishing always range from good to excellent. But as anglers, we know that isn't the way it is. When you talked about fishing to Jim—and Elsie, too—you always knew you were getting the straight information. No enhancement. No fluff. No salesmanship.

If the fishing was off, was slow, hadn't happened yet, wouldn't happen until we got rain or the streams warmed up, that's exactly what Jim and Elsie would tell you.

If a new line or rod or lure wasn't what the manufacturer claimed, Jim wouldn't mince words about it. And he might not even sell it to you.

If you asked for a specific piece of tackle, Jim would ask you how and where you planned to fish, and if he knew something else would work better, he'd tell you. Even if it meant less money in his pocket.

That's part of why we loved him.

I think something else we all admired about Jim was his relationship with Elsie, although it wasn't the kind of thing any of us talked about. While fishing often took a lot of us away from our spouses, fishing always seemed to be something that brought Jim and Elsie together. They made fishing trips together. They complimented each other on fish they had caught. They worked side by side year-round.

Quite simply, it was apparent they loved each other and respected each other. That's why it seemed you were part of a family when you walked into that back room at Jim's shop. It was family.

Jim's Bait offered something that is increasingly rare in the world today—a sense of community. At Jim's, the attitude was one of complete acceptance. Downtown businessmen in suits and topcoats shared coffee with laid-off construction workers. Green and eager college students listened to grizzled North Shore steelheaders. Women were as welcome, if not as common, as men.

The common denominator was fishing, and it didn't matter who you were. There was a chair for you. A cup of coffee for you. An audience for you.

There are a lot of places to buy tackle. There are quite a few places to buy bait. But there aren't many places where you can do those things and feel the sense of belonging that you felt at Jim's.

How can it be? How can it be that Jim will no longer be there in his baggy blue jeans and his heavy flannel shirt and his day-old stubble of whiskers? How can it be that this gentle man with so much fishing wisdom will no longer be there to set the record straight when the tales get a little too tall? And where are we going to find another one like him?

The answer, I'm afraid, is nowhere.

Margaret's River

She is up ahead, plowing through elbow-high jewelweed. The jewelweed is glistening with the precious night's dew, and it dampens the sleeves of her old blue windbreaker.

Margaret Appleby, 78, has made this hip-boot trudge before.

"There's a big hole up here I usually fall into," she says.

She shuffles on, wicker creel slung over one shoulder, a satchel of fishing tackle bouncing against a hip. With a battered yellow fishing rod, she knocks the alder branches and the undergrowth out of her way.

Margaret is making for a spot where she believes we'll be able to find some brook trout. "Specks," she calls them, as a lot of the old-timers do. Short for speckled trout.

Off to one side, we can hear the stream, one of sixty or so that flow into Lake Superior between Duluth and the

Canadian border. It will remain nameless, out of respect to both Appleby and the fish. But if you have chased brookies on streams, you know the kind of place Appleby is headed for.

We arrive there, finally, crashing through the last curtain of alders, emerging into the full sunlight of the August morning.

"Try it here," Margaret says, gesturing a skinny arm toward a turbulent pool below a log.

The spot is one of those that any brook-trout angler would look at and say, "This is the place."

The river, not a nightcrawler-cast wide, comes coasting along smooth and fast. It turns elastic as it slides over the log, and the bubbles dancing in the sun below are reminiscent of a brookie's flanks.

Margaret has been fishing this spot—and those downstream—for more than forty-five years, which is when she married Wilfred Appleby, a Duluth carpenter.

"Before we got married," Margaret said, "he had his pals he went fishing with. When we got married, he was going to go out fishing with them. I said, 'We're married now. I go along.' I'll be damned if I was going to stay home."

So, for the next twenty years or so, they went. They fished North Shore streams. They fished stocked brook-trout lakes. They caught a lot of brook trout.

"After work lots of times, we took off and went fishing the Lester [River]," she said. "We didn't get no monsters, but we got a few."

Wilfred died in 1966 at age sixty-eight. Margaret didn't think it was time to quit brookie fishing.

Now, pushing eighty, she can still put on a pair of hip boots and go. She appears to be made of pipe cleaners. There cannot be an ounce of fat on her. She wears vintage bifocals, and her gray hair seems to roam at will until subdued by her fishing hat.

The hat is a classic: a white, floppy-brimmed thing, stained by decades of use. The stitches that once provided backbone to the brim have mostly been set free, and the brim now undulates as it circles Margaret's head.

She wears a pair of blue jeans, a blouse, and the blue windbreaker buttoned to the top. Huge safety pins hold one blue-jean pocket shut, guaranteeing that her fishing license—wrapped in plastic—will stay there in case she goes "dunking."

"I've gone dunking many times," she says.

"Going dunking" is Margaret's term for something most stream anglers have done somewhere along the way—filling a pair of hip boots with stream water, sitting down unexpectedly in a cool stream, or floating away with the current.

Her voice is raspy, her words clipped. She knows what she wants, and she'll announce the next course of action. Sitting in the car, having arrived at a river, for instance, she'll say, "OK. We're gonna put on our hippers, and we're gonna go."

And we go.

Nobody has ever arrived at a speckled trout stream more prepared to fish than Margaret. Nobody.

She had brought along, for this single day of fishing, the following: three ancient rods, an ancient creel, a metal cooler, another cooler of nightcrawlers, two thermoses of coffee, a jug of water, a bag of sphagnum moss (gathered in her backyard), a landing net, her satchel of tackle, and a plastic bag of dry clothes.

"In case I go dunking," she says.

Oh, and a little lunch: ham sandwiches for two, tomatoes, hard-boiled eggs, watermelon, cantaloupe, cheese, and chocolate pudding.

She is playing line out now, drifting a whole nightcrawler in the pool below the log. She remains close to shore, a concession to wading legs that might not be as sure as they once were. She knows she can't get to the best water at this hole, but she wants to make sure it gets fished.

"Try over there," she says, aiming a skinny finger beyond at a downed tree. "I'll bet there's one over there in that dark water."

She's right. We have two handsome brookies on moss before we leave the hole, one of about eight inches, another of ten.

We work downstream for a couple of hours, working pools and riffles and eddies behind large rocks. It is moderately hard work, standing on greasy rocks, wading a quick river, fighting through the shoreside jungle on what may once have been a trail.

It is difficult to imagine what it must be like doing that at 78, when you have arthritis that makes it painful just to drive a car. Margaret does not complain.

If she gets snagged, she works it out herself. If she breaks off, she ties on a new hook herself, though it might take a few minutes.

"It's hell being half-blind and trying to tie on a hook," she says.

All of that is balanced, perhaps, by the memories she carries with her downstream.

Of a brookie taken from behind a familiar deadfall. Of lakes she and Wilfred blazed their way into. Of days so good it was hard to quit fishing.

She tells the stories not with wistfulness, but with a sense that today, or next weekend, could be that good.

Margaret is playing a fish now. The old Mitchell reel is ratcheting away as she cranks against the brookie's resistance.

The old yellow rod is bending gracefully out near the tip. She holds the rod high and winds the Mitchell until the fish—a seven-incher—is hers.

She unzips her satchel and gets out a pair of needle-nose pliers to remove the hook. She opens the creel—its lid held on by hinges of string—and slides the little guy onto a bed of moss.

There is no fanfare about any of this. How many times must she have put a brookie in that creel? How many times must she have reached in for another nightcrawler and impaled it—wriggling for mercy—on her hook? How many times must she have shaken the rod until the line hung right, then flipped the 'crawler into the fast water?

No telling.

We work on downstream through the day. There are mosquitoes to battle.

"Holy smokes! These bugs!" Margaret says. "I haven't got enough to spare, and they act like it's free."

There is water that fails to produce fish.

"Look at this beautiful water," she says. "There should be a thousand brookies in here."

There are snags in streamside trees to be worked free.

"That would make a saint swear," she says.

There are memories to fish.

"Now we're going to go down to our favorite spot," she says.

It's almost as if Wilfred is there, as if the two of them are still fishing together.

The favorite spot comes through again, with one speck for Margaret, one for her companion.

We kneel by the stream and clean them, soak the moss in stream water and lay the fish back on the moss.

"That'll keep 'em nice and cool," Margaret says. "Now, if we just go east, we'll hit an open area. It's a shortcut back to the car."

We do.

And it is.

The Frugal Fly Fisher

On a drippy Monday morning in May, Rueben Swenson sits astride his homemade fly-tying bench beneath a rain tarp and puts the finishing touches on a black Woolly Bugger.

Occasionally, he snips a piece of thread from the fishing fly with a small pair of scissors. Like most of Rueben's equipment, the scissors didn't come from a store.

"These came from my surgery, too," says Rueben, 50.

He's talking about his second heart-bypass surgery, the one in 1990 in which doctors replaced five arteries in his heart with strips of veins from his stocky legs.

"Before they put me under, I asked them to save me the scissors and hemostats," Rueben says matter-of-factly, holding up the Woolly Bugger for inspection.

A fly-fisherman, of which Rueben is a consummate example, can always use scissors and hemostats. Hemostats are stainless steel clamps used by anglers to remove hooks from the jaws of fish. A pair of hemostats hangs from Rueben's camouflage shirt now.

That 1990 surgery, and one in 1985 when Rueben had two arteries bypassed, have much to do with why the Mahtowa resident is camped here at Kimball Lake off the Gunflint Trail north of Grand Marais, on a Monday morning.

Rueben lives here, in a matter of speaking.

Unable to work, subsisting on Social Security disability payments, Rueben spends all summer fishing trout lakes along the Gunflint Trail. Come fall, he migrates to Arkansas, where the warm air is friendly to his heart and lungs. He parks his twenty-one-foot trailer at a federal campground and fishes trout streams in Arkansas all winter.

"I fish pretty near every day of the year," Rueben says.

While a lot of anglers would consider such an existence paradise, probably not many, when given Rueben's circumstances, would trade places with him.

He hasn't been able to work since 1986, the year, he says, "they put me out to pasture."

A gentle, resourceful man who could not remain bitter for long, he began adapting to his heart condition and to his newfound economic status. He has perfected the art of living on little, says his friend John Connolly of Cloquet. Connolly calls Rueben "the frugal fly fisher," and the nickname has stuck among members of the Arrowhead Fly Fishers, of which Rueben is president.

Rueben gets by on less than $8,000 a year, he says.

"My major expense is gas," he says. "My other big expense is medicine."

Medicare paid most of the cost of his two heart surgeries, but he paid off the deductibles and other noncovered expenses at $25 per month.

Divorced and the father of two grown children, Rueben lives simply.

"If he comes over wearing a new outfit and I ask him where he got it," says his sister, Cloquet's Jan Deppa, "he gets this little grin and says, 'GW.'"

GW stands for Goodwill.

Rueben approaches his fishing as conservatively as he manages his money. He rarely starts fishing before 10 A.M. and is able to fish for about three hours straight without tiring. He does almost all of his summer fishing from a Belly Boat—a sophisticated innertube through which an angler dangles his legs wearing neoprene waders. In Arkansas, he fishes streams by wading conventionally. That level of immersion seems to suit his remaining heart muscle.

"I always feel the best when I'm about waist-deep in water," Rueben says.

He isn't sure where he will fish on this May Monday. And it doesn't much matter. He has about fifteen lakes along the Gunflint he fishes regularly. All of them have drive-up access. He can no longer make the trek into more remote lakes where larger trout might lurk. His existence is nomadic, and he doesn't decide about tomorrow until tomorrow becomes today.

"Wherever I happen to be for that night, I sleep there that night," Rueben says. "I wake up the next morning and decide whether I want to go to another lake."

Today he has been joined by Karl Kaufman of Cloquet, a fellow member of the Arrowhead Fly Fishers. They eye the rain, then decide to put on their waders, load their Belly Boats, and drive to a nearby lake.

In minutes, they have assumed their amphibious existence and waddled into the lake. Propelled invisibly by flippers on their feet, they find their fishing holes and bring the air alive with satiny loops of fly line.

Few things can add to the beauty of a North Country lake in late May, but a fly fisher is one of them. Rueben is a good fly-caster, and it is a joy to watch him haul line and shoot his fly over the water's olive drab surface. The line is faintly green, and Rueben throws it against a backdrop of fresh-leafed popples on a steep ridge. Loons call. A woodpecker stakes out territory. An osprey wings overhead.

Rueben has not always lived so peacefully. Raised in Mahtowa, he moved to Northfield, Minnesota, and operated a restaurant there.

"I was chasing the almighty dollar," he says. "I burned myself out in fifteen years on that."

He moved back north to Mahtowa, worked as a milk inspector and a logger, and in his early 40s divorced.

"When I got divorced, I had very little money," he said. "I said, 'At least I've got my health.' Four months later, I didn't have my health, either."

He had his first bypass operation in January 1985 and lay around for four months, contemplating the rest of his life.

"My son, Eric, came over and said, 'Dad, we gotta go fishing.' I said, 'I can't go fishing. I can't walk down to the river.'"

"We went to the Baptism [River, near Finland]. I felt a lot better when I got out in the water. We caught a few trout, and I've felt better ever since."

He kept on fishing, and when his breath got short in Minnesota's winter, he kept going south until he could breathe easily. He fishes Arkansas from November to April, then migrates back north, fishing Wisconsin's Root River, Sioux River, and Brule River on his way to Mahtowa. He leaves his trailer there, and goes on north to the Gunflint in his pickup.

"What keeps him alive," says his friend Karl Kaufman, "is this kind of living. Otherwise, he'd be dead."

Rueben rarely gets bored, even fishing every day, because of his passion for fly-fishing and insatiable curiosity about the pursuit.

"I think you have to be a fly fisher to do it," he says, "because you can never learn enough about fly-fishing. I think you could get stale throwing Rapalas."

He isn't bitter about the lot he has drawn in life. But he says as much as he enjoys fishing, he would rather be working.

"I'd rather not be fishing," he says. "I'd rather be healthy. I'm resigned to the fact that this is the way it's going to be. So, I'm going to live life the best I can—healthwise, moneywise, friendwise."

Some days are made for catching trout, and others are not. Rueben and Karl are blanked this afternoon and again in two hours of evening fishing on another lake. Brook trout seem to be rising halfheartedly for some tiny midges, but it isn't enough of a meal to trigger a big feed.

Back at camp, Rueben and Karl talk fishing around a campfire. The camp is simple—Rueben's pickup, Karl's pint-sized trailer and a couple of picnic tables.

The talk turns to Rueben's frugality.

"People want to take him to Mall of America," Karl says. "But he says, 'Nah, I don't want to go there. Every store in there has a cash register.'"

Rueben avoids cash registers, especially those that ring up full retail prices.

His main fly rod is graphite. He picked it up for $28—on sale from $38—at a Wal-Mart in Arkansas. It works. Last winter, he landed a thirteen-pound brown trout on it. This spring, it helped him land a twelve-pound steelhead on the Root River.

He found two fly reels at a Bass Pro Shop down south that had been returned by their previous owners. One didn't work. He walked across the street to a reel repair shop, bought a part for it, and fixed it.

His waders are Hodgman neoprenes that another angler gave him because they leaked. New Hodgmans might run an angler a couple hundred bucks. Not Rueben.

"I paid $20 for the waders, and patched them with three tubes of Aqua Seal," he says. "I've got $20 in the waders and $12 in Aqua Seal."

They still work.

His truck is a rustless 1983 Ford with an extended cab. He bought it with 90,000 miles on it, and it now shows 168,000. Runs good. His 5-foot-7 frame fits nicely crosswise in the extended cab, where he sleeps. A pieces of mosquito netting is held over an open window with several magnets.

There is little in his outfit he hasn't made, found, been given, or bought cheap.

He got tired of pumping his Coleman stove, so he converted it to propane and now runs it off a twenty-pound tank of the gas.

He designed and made his portable fly-tying bench. It appears to be one-fourth of a picnic table—a stub of bench and a stub of tabletop. He's looking for three other fly fishers to build the same thing so when they camp together they'll have a full-size table.

His maps of Superior National Forest are encased in clear plastic covers that once held restaurant menus. His rod cases are hand-built from PVC plastic. He ties flies with parts of road-killed deer, chickens, rabbits, and squirrels.

Only occasionally does he depart from frugality.

"That cooler," he says with a rare scowl.

He points at a red-and-white cooler on a picnic bench.

"I had to have one that size to fit inside another frame I made. I paid $11.97 for it. There was a warranty inside of it. I threw the warranty away. I thought, 'What could break on a cooler?'"

"Two days later the handle broke."

It is the only time in twenty-four hours that Rueben's countenance is anything other than peaceful.

Other anglers—other people—like being around Rueben because his calm seems to be contagious.

"I see him as a real soothing type of person," says his sister, Jan. "You spend a day with him and he energizes you."

Karl, his companion for these few days, agrees.

"Rueben slows me down," he says. "I'm coming out of the rat race. I get around Rueben, and I slow down. I even talk slower."

The peace seems to be in Rueben for two reasons. One is the pace his heart condition imposes upon him. The other is a result of his having chosen a life that will allow him to keep on living as long as possible. He has had, perhaps, more opportunity than most to contemplate his own mortality. While there is no sense of morbidity about his prospects for longevity, Rueben has come to terms with his situation.

Sitting in his Belly Boat earlier that evening, with a full moon rising over the lake and no trout bothering his elk-hair caddis, Rueben spoke openly about his fishing life.

"I have two options," he says, line carving the cool night over his head. "I can sit at home, or I can sit here. I'd rather sit here."

All things being equal, he would just as soon be working, earning money, making what he calls a meaningful contribution to the world.

"This isn't totally meaningful," he says. "But where I am now, I'm grateful for the ability I have."

"I try not to think about my health. I'm not optimistic. I know someday this is going to take me down."

He makes few commitments into the next year. His kids are grown and on their own. He no longer has the dog that used to travel with him. He worried about what would happen to the dog if he died.

"I believe in God, and I feel like I've made my peace with him," Rueben says, waiting for a trout to sip his caddis. "If I go, my fishing partners will have to fish with somebody else."

The night is still for several moments. Rueben lifts his fly from the water, makes two false casts overhead and drops the offering lightly on the lake.

Somewhere off on another shore, Karl Kaufman is fishing. The two men have not spoken to one another for more than an hour.

Finally, in the silence, comes Rueben's gentle voice again.

"Had I been able to work, I probably wouldn't have to be the frugal fly fisher," he says. "But I don't know if I'd be any happier."

Shared Passions

There they go. The two newlyweds are skiing up Moose Lake on this March morning to a little brook trout lake.

That's Bob Cary, 76. He's the one carrying the frame pack with his fishing rods, his tackle, and his mukluks inside. He's on a pair of old skis, wearing a corduroy cap with a bill and earflaps, a Norwegian-print sweater, and ski-racing tights.

Out ahead, where she likes to be, is his new bride, Edie Sommer, 64. It's easy to pick her out. She's the one skiing without poles. She broke a few ribs earlier this winter—falling on a ski pole—and can't use her upper body much yet. She's under doctor's orders not to fall today.

Bob and Edie were married February 21. Between them they had had eighty-nine years of marriage already, so they knew what they were getting into. Bob's first wife, Lil, died several years ago after the couple had been married forty-six years. Edie's husband, Bob, died a couple of years ago after he and Edie had been married forty-three years.

Both Bob and Edie happen to love skiing, and pretty soon they happened to love each other. Now they're skiing together toward something else that Bob loves—brook-trout fishing.

The trout lake is about four miles as the ski glides from the public landing on Moose Lake. Four miles in, four miles out. A few hours of fishing.

Even without using ski poles, Edie leads the way. A mite of a human who can't weigh one hundred pounds, she won her age group (60 to 64) at the National Masters Ski Championships in 1994. She also won her age-group title in the Great American Ski Chase the same year. That was a series of six fifty-kilometer (thirty-one-mile) races. She knows how to ski.

She doesn't look much like a brookie angler in her black tights and a black turtleneck. What she looks like is a water strider as she skate-skis across the frozen surface of the lakes.

Bob has made this trip up the Moose Lake chain literally hundreds of times in the three decades he's lived on or near Moose Lake. First a canoe outfitter, now a newspaper editor, author, and illustrator, he has shagged trout, walleyes, bass, pike, and crappies out of more lakes than most of us will get to in one lifetime.

But his guiding has yet to impress his new bride. We're approaching the short portage into our trout lake when he proclaims to her, "I'll show you right where these trout are."

"You told me that three times last fall," she fires back.

On none of these occasions, Bob explains, did he produce a fish for his fiancée. Just a streak of bad luck, he says.

We have drawn a day beyond compare to make our trip. When we emerge on the lake, the March sun is beating down and the day is windless. We don't even bother to put on jackets or change into our mukluks.

Edie goes to her stash of Diet Coke, hauled along in the plastic bottles that are legal to carry in the Boundary Waters Canoe Area Wilderness. She twists off a top and takes a long pull on the bottle.

"I've got a thing about Diet Coke," she explains.

We drill several holes and begin getting bites almost immediately. None of the bites, however, materializes into an actual fish. Bob suspects we are being nibbled by the tiny brookies stocked just last fall in the lake at fingerling size.

"These are stockers. Little guys about five inches long," he says. "But it's good to feel a bite."

We feed them waxworms, whole dead minnows, and parts of dead minnows. But we cannot hook them on a Swedish Pimple or a Little Cleo.

"If we camp out here 'til year after next, they'll be keepers," Bob says.

It is one of the finest days to not catch fish any of us has ever known. The winter has not been difficult, but still, this warmth, the intensity of this sun, is something we seem to have forgotten from last summer.

To be honest, it is difficult to maintain any aggressiveness toward fishing. Mostly, we stand on the ice and tell stories of honeymoons and honey holes, Labrador retrievers and President Clinton, ski races and grandkids. We jig our minnows and waxworms halfheartedly, soaking up the sun. Yes, we're fishing. But as often happens when people are fishing, something more significant than the catching of fish occurs.

Listening to Bob and Edie, contemplating their lives at 76 and 64, someone in the middle of life cannot help feeling a sense of wonder. First, there's the fact that they've skied in here and will ski out, eight miles round-trip. No big deal.

I suspect this is because they have always done this. Always hiked and paddled and portaged, always run or skied or

skated. Neither Bob nor Edie has ever given any thought to
it. There were fish to catch. There were deer to hunt. There
were races to run. So, they went. They're still going—and
they're in good enough shape to keep going.

Now, given the surprising twists of life, they're doing these
things together. They had sometimes camped and fished the
canoe country together as a foursome with their first spouses.
Now, as Bob says, with Bob Sommer and Lil Cary looking
down on them from above, he and Edie are laughing and
traveling and fishing their way into this new life together.

You watch them, now sitting side by side on the lakeshore
at lunch, and try to imagine what your own future might
hold. You cannot help it. Each of us has this vision of how
our lives might play out. Surely Bob and Edie did, too. And
is this anything like they might have predicted? Sitting in the
March sun like a couple of high-school kids, laughing and
teasing and obviously appreciating each other? How could
either of them have ever seen this coming? How could they
have known it would be this good?

And how long might any of this last? How many brook
trout lakes? How many ski races? How many deer hunts?

When Bob bought his wedding ring for Edie, the jeweler
said he could engrave a few words inside of it. Bob said, "Whatever." He meant it. The jeweler engraved it. Edie loved it.

"It used to be everything was 'forever,'" Bob said. "Now
it's 'whatever.'"

They both seem to understand what that means in a
way that only someone who has lost a spouse and found
another understands.

Bob and Edie began talking about their wedding and
honeymoon, neither of which worked out exactly as they
had imagined. They almost didn't get married that day in
February. Their pastor suffered a head injury skiing the

Birkebeiner ski race that morning and was still a little woozy at the 5 P.M. ceremony in Duluth. But he managed to get Bob and Edie hitched.

The honeymoon was even more eventful. First, Bob and Edie's grown kids wanted to come up to the motel room with them and watch the Olympics that night, something the wedding couple hadn't had in mind. Both had the flu, and the next day Bob ended up in the emergency room of St. Mary's Medical Center with a bad case of bronchitis. Later, in a Florida motel, Bob broke his toe when he walked into Edie's suitcase in the night. And at another motel room on the honeymoon, the newlyweds found that the room they checked into was already occupied by someone else.

Now, back home, their broken bones are mending, and their lives have regained a sense of normalcy.

Finally, Bob brings us back to the prospect of fishing. We get serious enough to move across the lake for the afternoon fishing. It's here that I catch what will prove to be the only fish. It is beautiful, but it's not a brook trout.

It's a largemouth bass, a species that Bob suspects has moved in from an adjoining lake over the past several years. It's a classic largemouth: the extended lower jaw, the gaping mouth, the deep body, the dark green stripe along its lateral line. And all of that bassiness compressed into a fish no longer than two inches.

I suppose I should have released it, but Bob wanted a photo of it, and my Lab ate it shortly afterward.

The ski home is beyond warm. It is hot. Bob stops at one point to peel off his own cap, and beads of sweat glisten on his smooth scalp. He must think, at times like this, about all of the days he has come down this lake—in canoes, in boats, on skis, in big waves, at 40 below zero. He must think about all of the times the trout cooperated and all the times they did not.

But now he is watching Edie, out ahead of us, silhouetted against the lake. Lean and little, she looks as if she's made out of wire. Bob watches her moving along.

"How could a guy get so lucky twice in one lifetime?" he says.

He lets that thought drift around for a moment. We stand in the sun, amid the scent of pine needles, leaning on our ski poles and looking down the dazzling white lake.

"If they blow the whistle, tell me my time is up—hey, I've had a great trip," Bob says. "I've had a great trip."

Up ahead, Edie looks around, probably wondering what's holding us up.

Travels with Charlie

This is not just another small walleye. That much is clear by the way the tip of Charlie Banks's fishing rod keeps plunging into the water of this border-country lake.

Something stout is on the other end of that line.

Charlie, 73, is laughing his high-pitched laugh again, throwing back his head and holding his rod against the fish's determined charges.

"And I got a knot in my line," he laments from the middle of the canoe.

The big northern pike fights from the depths for a couple of minutes, trying to throw the hook. Charlie's rod nearly doubles beneath the canoe, and, a second later, the pike throws itself clear of the water on the other side of the craft.

Amazingly, the fish remains on the line. Charlie plays it for another eternity until suddenly the line goes limp. The

game is over. The line has broken. Maybe it was the knot that
weakened the line. Or maybe the northern finally got its toothy
maw on the light monofilament.

In either case, Charlie is not heartbroken. He utters not a
single disparaging word. He doesn't hang his head. It takes a
lot more than that to get Charlie Banks down.

"That was fun," he'll say later, back at our camp among
the red pines.

Charlie's encounter with the northern pike will be cata-
logued with all the other memories from this annual May
trip he makes to the Boundary Waters Canoe Area Wilderness with his friend Mark Helmer, 44. The two are fast friends
and close neighbors in the Clover Valley area between Duluth and Two Harbors.

It is because of Mark, who has been making this spring
trip since the mid-1970s, that Charlie is still coming to the
canoe country.

"I was in my mid-60's, and Mark told me I had to go 'til
I was 70," Charlie says.

At 73, he's more than fulfilled that commitment. When we
headed down the Nina Moose River north of Ely for this mid-
May trip, Charlie was the first one down the portage. He hustled
off down the trail carrying a Duluth Pack, a couple of canoe
paddles, and a fistful of fishing rods. Even under that load, he
traveled with the same energetic bounce that characterizes his
stride on the ski trails. He has been one of Duluth's outstand-
ing cross-country skiers for the past several decades.

Six portages later, we pitched our tents on a jutting pen-
insula at the east end of Lac La Croix, a meandering lake that
lies on the Minnesota-Ontario border. Joining Mark and
Charlie were Mark's longtime friend Rick Francisco of
Hermantown, Roger Pekuri of Ely, and I.

Mark will tell you there are two reasons for making this
trip in mid-May, just after the Minnesota fishing opener.

"Bugs and people," he says.

Or, more accurately, the absence of both. The canoe country is relatively untraveled this time of year, and the mosquitoes and blackflies don't make their appearance until late May.

The trip has a single focus: fishing. We have come with minnows by the quart, a jugful of leeches, a bag of potatoes, several loaves of bread, and two coolers—one for oxygen-packed minnows on the way in, one with ice for fillets on the way home.

Mark and Charlie share Mark's twenty-foot Kevlar canoe, and the other three of us rotate through its third seat each day. Most of the fishing will be with jigs and minnows, although Charlie always fishes the same way, using two split-shot sinkers and a plain hook with a minnow on it. He catches his share of fish.

Charlie sits in the canoe's middle seat, tended by Mark in stern and, on this first day, Rick in the bow. When Charlie catches a walleye, Mark or Rick lands it and puts it on the stringer. When Charlie needs a new minnow, someone grabs one for him.

"They say to take a kid fishing," Charlie will say later. "You guys take an old man fishing."

Mark considers it a privilege to do so. He and Charlie have forged their friendship grooming ski trails together at Korkki Nordic, the ski trails Charlie carved out of the woods forty years ago. The two men have built a chalet there and a sauna. This summer, they plan to put up a canoe shed.

The depth of their friendship is evident throughout the trip, both in the canoe and in camp, as Mark checks in with his senior partner.

"How ya' doin', Charlie?"

"How's your back, Charlie?"

"Ready for coffee, Charlie?"

When Charlie needs a split shot taken off his line, he asks Mark for assistance.

"Nothing to it, partner," Mark says.

And when Mark sets the hook on another walleye, it's Charlie leading the cheers.

"Attaboy, Mark," he says.

As if he know his time with Charlie may have an outside limit, Mark guards it carefully.

"Some guys at work wanted me to go on a trip Memorial Day weekend," Mark says, "but I don't go on a trip without my partner."

The fishing is decent, if not fast, that first evening. Roger fools a three-pound walleye on a tiny Cicada. Mark gets a four-pounder on a red jig. Most of the larger fish are tossed back. A few smaller ones will go into the cooler overnight for the next afternoon's fish fry.

The days are structured for fishing. Up at seven or so. Breakfast of hashed browns and scrambled eggs. Out to fish until two or so. Fish dinner about four. Out to fish again until sunset.

The trip is cold for May in Minnesota. Snow falls one morning. Wind finds us nearly everywhere we fish. Each plunge into the minnow bucket for a fresh chub means an aching hand.

"Getting a minnow out is like shock therapy," Mark says.

Still, the days are filled with the sweet surprises that color any trip into the back country. A beaver sunning itself on top of its lodge. An otter curious about our passing. A purple finch that lands on Charlie's cap as he sits before the afternoon fire.

Time in camp is laced with hot coffee, good fires, and well-told stories. It is the stories, as much as the fishing, that come to be the fabric of this kind of trip.

We are gathered around the fire one afternoon, trading tales from Quebec and Alaska and the Northwest Territories, when Rick says what we've all been thinking.

"This is what I've been waiting for for about six months," he says. "Sitting in front of this fire."

Sometimes Charlie will disappear quietly from camp and be gone for some time. He'll reemerge from the woods later, hauling a length of red pine or a long-dead spruce. Then he and Mark will each get on one end of the saw and make some wood.

When a fire needs to be built, chances are Charlie will already have it kindled. The coffee pot goes on, positions are taken up, and we wait for Mark to fry a pyramid of walleye fillets for supper.

"This is fun," Rick says at one point. "I couldn't do this all the time, but I could do it the majority of the time. At least 52 percent."

Mark has served up the fillets one afternoon, and a silence falls over the camp as each of us digs in. The fire is warm. The fillets are light and crisp. In the distance, all we see is sky and forest and water.

"This," Mark offers softly, "would be my idea of going to heaven."

The fishing, with no help from the weather, is tough. We catch walleyes every day, and a few huge crappies. But we work for our fish, taking them where we can find them, settling for smaller ones than the trip usually produces. Every day we have more walleyes than five men can eat, and we'll have fillets to bring home, too.

Throughout the trip, those of us in our 40s quietly marvel at Charlie. There is among us an unspoken wonder about what our futures will hold, if we'll be climbing in and out of a canoe at 73, if we'll know anyone in his 40s who'll want to have us along.

We know, from having lived a little while ourselves, just how fickle this jaunt through life can be, how little it takes to cut short an activity that one has come to love. A bum leg will do it. A bad heart. Fingers that won't tie knots anymore.

We try to stay in shape as a hedge against those demons. But in our hearts we all know part of it is just luck. The cards we were dealt. Choices made long ago. Fate itself. We are given hope when we see Charlie beating the odds, at 73, here on La Croix one more time.

For Rick and Roger and me, there is also an awe of sorts about the friendship Mark and Charlie have cultivated across a generation. It has its roots in the Korkki ski trails and their common Finnish heritage, but it goes beyond that. It's part father-son, part man-to-man, part fishing buddies. The friendship works because Charlie is as gracious in receiving Mark's assistance as Mark is genuine in offering it.

We're sitting around the fire one evening when, for a fleeting moment, Mark and Charlie allow themselves to consider future May trips to La Croix.

"Charlie's three years beyond his pledge," Mark says. "I made him promise he'd go on these trips until he was 70."

"I don't know if I can keep going much longer," Charlie says. "You see how slow I get out of the canoe at the end of the day?"

"Aw, now Charlie," Mark says.

A long silence comes over the camp. Our thoughts are lost in the column of woodsmoke before us. For several moments, none of us allows his gaze to wander far from the fire.

The Longest Season

Winter and Water

Dropping onto the frozen river is like being delivered to another world. The one above hisses with cars and southbound snow machines swaddled on their trailers.

This one—the river world—is white and narrow and nearly silent. It's the Sucker River on a five-below-zero morning in early February. Descending into it, on skis, one is immediately welcomed into a valley of quiet. The river is a ribbon of white bordered by spruce and fir, a few pines, and, in places, walls of sheer rock.

What the river will give you on a morning like this is solitude, a few quick thrills on skis—and ice. Beautiful, uncommon, continuously changing ice.

By all accounts, this hasn't been much of a winter in the north. Too mild. Too snowless. Too wimpy.

All in all, a wonderful respite.

Yet there has been plenty of winter by river standards. Plenty of ice to support a skier and a yellow dog. And plenty of the kind of ice that makes skiers stop, lean on their ski poles, and stare for long, silent moments.

Double-layer ice with ice spindles connecting the two plates. Dripping finger ice at the lips of rapids. Long, transparent ovals of black ice with the river bubbling away below.

There's more. Bulbous, cloudy waterfall ice with serious gurgling somewhere beneath it. Beaded, silver jewelry ice bordering an open-water riffle. Mean shark-tooth ice beneath a hanging shelf of shorefast ice.

And fat, lumpy extrusions of bank ice formed by all-winter seeps or warm-weather runoff. Some of it is gray, and some of it is stained the color of tea by deposits of soil.

All of this ice changes week to week, and sometimes day to day, as a result of fresh snowfall, extreme cold, or daytime thaws. Occasionally it will change in a matter of seconds under the weight of a skier, and his or her companions will go home with a story to tell. These rivers are shallow, and the stories are usually of wet feet, sometimes of wet legs, and always of silly grins.

Under some conditions—the right combination of cold and humidity, perhaps—the river will make rime ice. This is the ultrawhite ice that forms in tiny shards along the edges of jewel ice or stalactite ice or spindle ice. Sometimes it affixes itself to the sharks' teeth and sometimes to the underside of a shorefast plate of ice.

It is delicate and beautiful.

A similar ice—superwhite, in shardlike flakes—forms atop smooth, clear ice at times. In places the clear ice is dappled with these circular white etchings, each the size of a quarter. These clusters look like some odd albino lichen clinging to a huge piece of obsidian.

Maybe if one lived on the river and watched it every day, he would know how the river makes this elaborate menu of ice. But for the skier who just drops in for a day, it is enough just to shuffle and marvel.

Beyond the ice, river skiing offers other ways to embrace winter. There is climbing to be done along the way, too, as one ascends the river. All of it on the Sucker, at least for now, can be done with skis on. There are rivers—and conditions—that call for the removal of skis and a commitment to some high-level clambering. None of that on this morning.

Many have been here, done this. Once can see their tracks in various stages of preservation. Snowshoers. Other skiers. Somebody on foot, not long ago, judging by the sharpness of his boot tracks.

The climbing goes smoothly. Up the river. Past the "Beware of Dog" sign where no trace of a dwelling is apparent. Past the little mustard-colored cottage. Up to where one finds a hint of the river's origins, in the flats, where the river courses slowly out of the bog country.

And then the return trip. Down. The ride toward Lake Superior is by turns a gentle joy, a carnival ride, and—when reason prevails—a controlled slide involving skis, buns, and elbows.

It is best to have done all of one's ice watching on the trip up because the downbound skier is preoccupied with an overwhelming dose of giddiness.

The descent is always over too soon.

If a skier is truly addicted to this ice-intensive experience, he can be thinking only one thing as he climbs back to the highway.

So many rivers. So little winter.

The Old Boys on the Bay

The old boys were at it again over on Chequamegon Bay the other day. Some young boys, too, but this was a weekday, and mostly it was the old-timers.

They were sitting there, monklike, in their canvas ice-fishing shelters, communing with the trout. They were trying to get the trout to commune back on the business ends of some Jiggin' Raps and Swedish Pimples and other assorted limitations of baitfish.

As was my custom, I moseyed from tent to teepee to those commercial pop-up jobs, communing with the anglers. The fishing was slow. That's what the old boys said. Slow.

Anglers don't ever say the fishing is bad. Rarely will they call it poor. Slow is about as bad as it ever gets.

It occurred to me as I made my rounds that in spite of the fishing, these guys were happy. They weren't ecstatic, no. But

they were undeniably happy. Sort of a peaceful happy. Kind
of a quiet happy.

Here was this tiny community of ice-anglers, most of them
not catching fish, and everyone happy. I thought about it.

Well, it didn't take too much thinking for it to start making sense. They might not have been catching many fish, but
they were out on the ice of the world's broadest freshwater
lake. They were sitting quietly, bathed in soft light. They were
free to think whatever thought might choose to form under
their stocking caps and parka hoods.

Hey, people have been known to attend church for a lot
of those same reasons, wearing clothes not nearly as comfortable. I studied on it a little longer.

These guys had found a way to do something that most
of us find all too rare in our lives—spend some reflective time
alone. They were free to contemplate the great mysteries—
life, death, the molecular tenacity of ice, and whether the
time had come to put on a new minnow.

It is a free person who can cogitate on things so great
and small, his thoughts caressed by the soft hiss of the stove
at his feet.

There are no reports to be completed here, no snowblow-
ers begging for an oil change, no daughters to be retrieved
from day care. No tax forms to pick up, no bank deposits to
be made, no bills to be paid. No dog to be walked, no news to
watch, no milk to pick up.

There is only the green water, the filtered light, and the
occasional talking of the ice.

And, of course, the possibility that a trout might inhale a
Pimple at any moment and become dinner a few moments later.

Oh, yes. The fishing.

Whatever happened, the fishing was not going to get any
worse. It could only continue the same or get better. And if

ever an optimist was born, it was the ice-angler. Consider the possibilities: The fishing was probably good yesterday, and therefore could be good today. There is a front moving in that could turn the fish on. The fishing has been slow, and therefore the fish are due to bite. The guy at the bait shop said this was the hot bait. The fish usually hit best between 2:30 and 4:30, and it's 2:00 now.

Optimism is right behind solitude in the ice-angler's world.

I moved from hut to hut, getting the same report.

"Slow."

"Pretty quiet."

"A little slow."

And I kept talking to happy people. I almost hated to intrude, they seemed so content before I came shuffling up to their zippered tent doors.

Yep. Things were slow on Chequamegon Bay the other day.

Slow—and good.

Deep Trouble

Rats.

That's what we are.

Rats, crawling around in a white maze. This last blizzard did it to us. Finally consigned us to this life of scurrying about in labyrinthine corridors of snow.

On foot, we shuffle down alabaster hallways that once were mere sidewalks. Our grocery bags ricochet off snowblown cliffs. Our toddlers, trundling along behind us, swipe mittenfuls of sedimentary snow harboring impurities three snowstorms old.

In cars, the going is even worse. We scuttle around town, nosing out from intersections like small rats afraid the alpha male will whip past and mash us into oblivion. We are tentative and edgy. We poke our hood ornaments from our private tunnels, hoping other drivers will see us—and swerve—before they peel our grills off.

A while back, in our town, there was a big fuss about residents clearing their sidewalks. I could clear my sidewalk, all right—if I had a D-9 Caterpillar. All I have is an eight-horsepower Ariens. That elongated pyramid of snow the city plowed onto my sidewalk looks down at my Ariens and laughs.

I know there are those who depend on sidewalks to get around. I don't mean to make light of this. But this is bigger than all of us. We are just rats down here. Our option to dig new raceways in our subsnow world has expired.

"I gave up on my sidewalk a long time ago," a man I know said. "I just put a pair of snowshoes out in my yard. If people need 'em, they can put 'em on."

Assuming you can edge out into the streets to drive, a whole new set of rules applies. If you meet someone on a side street, one of you is going to have to careen up on the snowbank to let the other one pass.

Four-lane thoroughfares have been reduced to one and a half lanes in each direction. Those stripes on the street mean nothing now. It's every driver for him- or herself. Give and take. Dodge and weave. You see two cars ahead of you trying to squeeze side by side into one and a half lanes, and you fear the worst—interlocking side mirrors. Imagine it—two cars suddenly fused like Siamese twins of steel, coursing the avenues in tandem, each struggling for steerage.

That's the way it is these days, in the maze we call home. We skitter around like so many entrenched rodents, feeling our way, making our feeble probings, selecting our best options, and hoping. That's all we can do.

Every once in a while—amazingly—we solve the maze, tap the bar that lets down the food, reinforcing our small brains to keep trying again and again.

Rats.

In the grand experiment we call winter in the North.

Webbed Feet

The first hill leads straight to the moon. The trail rises precipitously, and at its crest the quarter-moon reclines in the night sky like a shard of porcelain. I huff along in silence on my snowshoes, using a pair of ski poles for both balance and propulsion. The dog is ahead of me somewhere, and now she comes bounding back to check in, sliding up to the tips of my snowshoes like an otter out of control. Assured that I'm all right, she reverses direction in a silent explosion of snow and is gone again into the night.

It feels just right to be here, on snowshoes. The cross-country skiing has been superb throughout December, but five or six inches of fresh snow have fallen earlier this day, and I've pulled out the snowshoes for the first time this winter.

When I reach the moon, I turn east and tramp along to a familiar bluff. It overlooks much of the Duluth neighborhood where I live, and soft light from porches and windows glows in the hush below me. Moving on, I shuffle to another promontory in this one-thousand-acre woods.

Below us, in a pool of light, three boys smack a puck back and forth on a hockey rink. I watch their dark forms gliding on the ice and listen to one of the defining sounds of a Duluth winter night: the slap of hockey sticks on ice and the smack of a puck against the rink's boards.

But it is silence and the night we have come for, so the dog and I turn and backtrack to a trail I know. It leads us along a ridge of oaks and birches. The trees stand like naked sentinels in the moonlight, their branches reaching for the first stars we've seen in several nights.

The woods glisten in silver light. The trees are silver. The snow is silver. The dog is silver. I move along with near-silent footsteps. The snow is full of air, and each webbed footfall displaces all of the fresh snow. The snowshoes find the firm base of previous snows below, and the going is good. Cruising along, I inhale the thin air, appreciate constellations, and admire the undulation of shadows on the snow.

The exhilaration that accompanies the speed of cross-country skiing is addicting, but there is something compelling about traveling in this time-proven way. One measured step at a time. You are free to meander wherever your whimsy leads you. You move slowly enough to look around without fear of toppling over. You work hard enough to feel as if you're doing something good for yourself.

I am reminded again, traveling at night, that we two-leggers are hopelessly diurnal in nature, which is to say we are a lot better at getting around in the day than at night. We do a lot after darkness falls, but very little without the aid of artificial light.

I have to learn again that the best way to see something at night is to look just to one side of it. Something about the rods and cones of our eyes, I believe.

But mostly, it is the dog that points up the tremendous difference in the way we embrace the night. She bounds around as if we were in broad daylight, always finding the trail without problem, never careening into trees or low-hanging branches. I, on the other hand, must look hard to discern the trail, depend on my ski poles for decent balance, and strain to make the dark shape ahead materialize into a stump.

I remember dogsledders saying that their teams seem to prefer running in the dark and often pick up the pace a bit after sunset. I imagine deer and foxes moving through these woods in the silver light. They must think it nothing unusual.

For about an hour, we wander through the night. Once, I pause on an open bluff and let the raw northwest wind sting my face. I remember standing on the same ridge one September afternoon when the hawks were migrating, watching a sharpshin slice past at eye level not far away. But it's December now, and the sharpshins are eating mice in Missouri. We turn and find the path we have broken on our way in and follow it downhill, bathed in silver light.

Friendship Fires

I went to the woods because I needed to be alone and to see some white snow.

Most of the snow I had seen lately was brown. City snow. Greasy stuff, mixed with sand and salt and grunge.

So I loaded up the snowshoes and the mukluks, and I took off. I didn't know where I was going to go, and it didn't much matter. All I wanted to do was walk or shuffle along, let the northwest wind pepper my face, and let my legs get tired.

Sometimes that kind of an outing is just what we need. We don't need to catch anything. We don't need to hunt anything. We don't need to pursue anything.

We just need to get out, stomp around, get wet or cold or weary, and come home again, renewed.

I remember a time when I was a kid, maybe 16. My younger brother grabbed his .410 shotgun, threw on a couple of hooded sweatshirts, and headed for the back door. It was a howling, blustery day in December. Cold, too.

"You're not going hunting, are you?" my mom asked Jim.

"I'm going out to get my face hard," he said.

And he walked out the door into the unforgiving day.

I have always remembered that because I knew exactly what he was feeling. What he was saying was that it didn't matter whether he came across a cottontail rabbit or a bobwhite quail, or if he got a shot at either one. What he wanted to do was get out and march around and let the elements work him over.

I cannot say where that feeling comes from, but I know when it's building inside me, and I know what cures it.

A walk in the woods.

The dog and I left the highway behind us and walked down the trail. Someone had been there before us sometime during the recent thaw, and their refrozen tracks made a tough trail to follow. For me, anyway. The dog was off tapping her nose into deer tracks.

The trail crossed a small creek, which we followed on some questionable ice until the creek joined a river. The ice wasn't questionable in the river. It simply wasn't there in a lot of places.

We climbed a steep bank and moved along the river, upstream. I knew the river from earlier encounters, and I knew a nice set of falls was just around a shoulder of rhyolite rock.

The falls were right where I had left them last time, but a big piece of clay shoreline had slumped down to the river, and now a huge cedar hung over the falls. Enough of its roots were still in the soil that I figured it would keep living, which means that when we ski the river later in the winter, we'll have to be ducking when we careen down that set of frozen falls.

We moved on upstream.

The day was giving me everything I wanted. The temperature was in the teens, and the windchill was probably below zero. Even down in the river valley, my ears felt better with the flaps down on my cap.

The birches were white and the sky was blue, and it felt just right to be padding along in a pair of mukluks. You can feel the snow in mukluks, and the lay of the land. You feel like a kid hopping around in a pair of pajamas with feet in them, which, near as I can recall, was a good way to feel.

All I had brought with me in my pack was a small piece of closed-cell foam to sit on and some matches. I gathered some downed wood—cedar and spruce and alder. I built the fire on the edge of the river, in a splash of sunshine.

I have built a hundred little fires like that one. Friendship fires, a friend of mine calls them. I had nothing to cook over the fire, not even a pot in which to heat tea water. But I knew I needed to sit by that fire and smell it, and listen to the sounds it made.

I remember when I was new to this country, and a friend and I would take off on pokearounds for the day. He knew the country, and I was soaking up everything he could tell me about it. We would stop for lunch and kindle a fire and toast sandwiches over it.

Now, every time I build a friendship fire, I think about those days and the country we covered. The memories come flooding back with the first whiff of wood smoke that rises from the birchbark and small twigs.

Sitting there, listening to the cedar snap in my fire, I recalled another fire I built in the Ely country one day. A friend

and I had caught several walleyes on a lake we had all to ourselves one morning, but had gotten chilly and decided to go
ashore to boil up some tea.

We had a pot hung from a stick over the fire, and we were
enjoying the warmth when we noticed a canoe out on the
lake. We were surprised to see anyone else on the lake—but
as it turned out, nobody else was on the lake.

It was our canoe, out there with our stringer of walleyes,
drifting peacefully down the lake. I lost the flip and had to
swim, and the fire felt even better after that.

I thought about those days, and a lot more, as I nursed
the fire along last week. When it had burned down to the
rocks below and I was out of wood, I held my hands out to
its warmth one more time. Then I kicked snow on it and
padded back down the river, a different person than the one
who had hiked in.

Sam Cook has been the outdoors writer for the *Duluth News-Tribune* since 1980. His travels have taken him to Hudson Bay by canoe, dogsledding in the Northwest Territories, and paddling the Quetico-Superior wilderness. He is the author of *Camp Sights, Quiet Magic,* and *Up North,* all available from the University of Minnesota Press. He lives with his family in Duluth, Minnesota.